JOHANN SEBASTIAN
BACH

CLASSIC *f*M LIFELINES

JOHANN SEBASTIAN
BACH

AN ESSENTIAL GUIDE
TO HIS LIFE AND WORKS

CHRISTOPHER HEADINGTON

PAVILION

First published in Great Britain in 1997 by
PAVILION BOOKS LIMITED
26 Upper Ground, London SE1 9PD

Copyright © Pavilion Books Ltd 1997
Front cover illustration © The Lebrecht Collection

Edited and designed by Castle House Press, Penarth, South Wales
Cover designed by Bet Ayer

A CIP catalogue record for this book is available
from the British Library

ISBN 1 86205 026 0

Set in Lydian and Caslon
Printed and bound in Great Britain by Mackays of Chatham

2 4 6 8 10 9 7 5 3 1

This book can be ordered direct from the publisher.
Please contact the Marketing Department.
But try your bookshop first.

Contents

A NOTE FROM THE EDITORS

A biography of this type inevitably contains numerous references to pieces of music. The paragraphs are also peppered with 'quotation marks', since much of the tale is told through reported speech.

Because of this, and to make things more accessible for the reader as well as easier on the eye, we decided to simplify the method of typesetting the names of musical works. Conventionally this is determined by the nature of the individual work, following a set of rules whereby some pieces appear in italics, some in italics and quotation marks, others in plain roman type and others still in roman and quotation marks.

In this book, the names of all musical works are simply set in italics. Songs and arias appear in italics and quotation marks.

CHAPTER 1
CHILDHOOD AND SCHOOLDAYS
(1685–1703)

- ♦ Musical precociousness
- ♦ Death of his parents
- ♦ Studies in Lüneburg

Challenge anyone to name three of the greatest classical composers, and the chances are that Johann Sebastian Bach will be among them. Along with Beethoven and Mozart, he is almost a household name and his music has even featured as the theme for a TV commercial, the 'Air on the G string', from his *Third Orchestral Suite* happily accompanying the scene of a man contentedly smoking a Hamlet cigar – whose brand name reminds us of another cultural giant, Shakespeare.

Was Bach the Shakespeare of music? Not really, for against the Englishman's wide-ranging plots, characteristic of an imaginative inheritor of Renaissance ideas, Bach's is a far more closely focused world centring on his own time and the north-German society in which he lived, with its princes, prelates and poverty. Indeed, his music reflects his whole career as a working musician in courts and churches. Unlike his great German contemporary Handel, born in the same year, Bach composed no operas, although his treatment of the Passion story in his *St Matthew Passion* is as dramatic as anyone could wish, and while Handel became a wealthy impresario and remained a bachelor, Bach was never his own master and took on heavy family responsibilities. Thus, although he must have written his six *Brandenburg Concertos* partly for his own pleasure, they were also composed for the court orchestras of his employers Duke Wilhelm of Weimar and Prince Leopold of Anhalt-Cöthen, and then dedicated to yet another nobleman in whose court they were apparently not played at all. Similarly, his composition of over three hundred church cantatas may have been enjoyable work, but writing them was also his duty as an organist and choirmaster in several Lutheran churches, culminating in his final and longest-lasting appointment as a *Kantor* at Leipzig who provided and directed the music of the city's principal churches.

His background was both ordinary and extraordinary. Ordinary, because his family was far from wealthy, and extraordinary because its profession was music. Even before he was born, on 21 March 1685, his was the greatest family of German musicians of the eighteenth century. The *New Grove Dictionary of Music and Musicians* lists around eighty Bachs, beginning with men such as Hans Bach (c.1555–1615), a violinist and entertainer at the ducal court of Württemberg. There is a picture of him with a fiddle in one hand and what may be a roll of music in the other (it could be a drinking cup), and it was said of him, 'When you hear him you have to laugh.'

Sebastian's father, Johann Ambrosius Bach, was a church organist and violinist in the town of Eisenach in Thuringia, around a hundred miles to the west (and slightly south) of Leipzig. A respected 'municipal musician' who belonged to a players' guild, he played twice a day at the town hall and also acted as an assistant to his cousin Johann Christoph Bach, the organist of St George's Church. Sebastian's mother Maria was the daughter of a furrier.

This sounds a secure background. Yet Sebastian was born in an age when health and longevity were not to be taken for granted. He was one of eight children, but only four of them survived into adulthood, and his mother died in May 1694. His father remarried later in the year, for he could hardly bring up his children alone, but then he too died, in February 1695. His widow applied to the Eisenach town council for help, but little came her way and the family was broken up. Thus, by the age of nine Sebastian had lost his parents and also his home.

However, his father had given him his first instruction in music, both in keyboard and violin playing, and after three years' attendance at a good grammar school, the Lateinschule, he was already showing promise and strength of character. After he had lost both parents, his oldest brother Johann Christoph, already a professional musician at twenty-four and the principal organist of the nearby town of Ohrdruf, took him in and became his musical mentor. It was now that his special talent became increasingly evident on the keyboard instruments of the time, namely the organ, harpsichord and clavichord. His brother found him an apt pupil, and also began teaching him the basic skills of composition. The boy sang, too, as a chorister in his brother's church and so earned a small salary, which helped pay for his keep.

The only problem may have been his sheer precocity. He became interested in a set of new keyboard compositions in his brother's library, but Johann Christoph thought them too advanced for him and locked them away. By some accounts, he then started to get up at night to prise them through the latticed front of the locked bookcase and copy them secretly, but was discovered by his brother and had his manuscript confiscated, only getting it back later, perhaps when he left his brother's home.

Sebastian stayed in Ohrdruf for five years, attending the Lyceum, a strict but well-regarded school, where he studied, among other things, Lutheran orthodoxy, Latin, history and mathematics, and seemingly excelled among his fellows. It has been claimed that he was always a year or more younger than his classmates, but this may be a pious exaggeration. However, on 15 March 1700, six days before his fifteenth birthday, he left his brother's home and moved to a new school in Lüneburg, a town not far from Hamburg and some two hundred miles to the north of Ohrdruf. There were probably several reasons for the move: Johann Christoph now had two children of his own and his wife was expecting a third, so that living, as he did, in a smallish cottage, he could hardly continue to accommodate his teenage brother. At the same time Sebastian was probably ready to seek wider horizons, and seems to have been influenced by one of his schoolmasters at the Lyceum, Elias Herda, who had himself been educated at the Lüneburg school, St Michael's.

The school was linked to a church, the Michaeliskirche, and was for commoners, including poorer boys with good voices such as Bach himself. With an older schoolfriend from Ohrdruf who probably accompanied him on his journey, Sebastian joined one of the two church choirs, the *Mettenchor* or Matins choir. In return, he was given free schooling, board and lodging and a share of fees earned at weddings and other such occasions. Although his treble voice may have broken fairly soon after his arrival, he continued to sing and became a 'choir prefect'.

At the same time, he continued his general studies and among his subjects were religious instruction (Lutheranism), Latin, mathematics, history and geography, German poetry and the physical sciences. But music remained his chief interest and skill, and he developed what was to become a lifelong interest in organs and organ building. He must have been pleased to find that the church's extensive music library, founded in 1555, contained words by other members of the Bach family, including his Eisenach uncle, Johann Christoph Bach. Still more importantly, its thousand volumes represented the work of nearly two hundred composers. Some of them were of the German school, ranging from Heinrich Schütz (1585–1672) to Dietrich Buxtehude (1637–1707), Danish-born but now one of Germany's most celebrated organists. But there was also music of other countries with correspondingly different styles. Although we do not know what access Sebastian had to this material, he may have seen and studied works by such major musicians as the Netherlander Orlande de Lassus (1532–94), a master of vocal polyphony, and Claudio Monteverdi (1567–1643), the great Italian composer of operas and madrigals.

It was also at this time that Sebastian got to know and appreciate the music of George Böhm, the organist at another Lüneburg church. This energetic musician and skilful composer much admired the organist Johann Adam Reincken, who occupied a church post in Hamburg and was now nearly eighty. Prompted by Böhm and perhaps accompanied by him, Sebastian more than once made the journey to Hamburg to hear Reincken play, necessarily travelling on foot and taking a day or more to cover the thirty miles or so. Once there, he may have stayed with his cousin, Johann Ernst Bach.

On one such occasion, he sat enraptured as the aged Reincken improvised at the excellent Catharinenkirche organ on the hymn melody '*By the Waters of Babylon*.' He also probably heard some performances at the Hamburg opera house, which was later to attract the talents of the young Handel. According to a story that his children told in later years, he was once returning alone from Hamburg to Lüneburg and, exhausted, sat down outside an inn, wishing that he had the money to go in and eat. Suddenly, someone threw out two herrings' heads which fell in front of him. On picking them up he found a gift of Danish coins inside, which allowed him to satisfy his hunger and thirst and left enough over for another visit to Hamburg.

Thus, these teenage years in Lüneburg were of immense value to the gifted youth with his willingness and ability to learn all he could from differing musical sources. Another inspiration came through the Ritteracademie, a companion school to St. Michael's, where wealthier boys learned such social arts as fencing, dancing and speaking French. The dancing master there was Thomas de la Selle, a Frenchman and a former pupil of the French composer Lully. He was also a violinist in a largely French orchestra at the ducal court of Celle, some fifty miles away, to which a French-born duchess had brought much of her native culture. After befriending Sebastian, de la Selle took him there several times to hear French dance music in the duke's small private theatre, and he may even have joined in as a violinist. In the chapel, he heard French organ music played by a French musician, Louis Gaudon, and elsewhere at court he heard and liked the harpsichord music of François Couperin (1668–1733), then still a young man but later to be a major figure in French music, enjoying a little rondeau by him enough to make a personal copy and noting down some of the grace notes and ornaments that made French keyboard music lighter and more decorative than German.

At around the time of his seventeenth birthday in 1702, Sebastian left Lüneburg and returned to his native Thuringia. The two years at St Michael's, together with his other musical experiences, had fitted him for the professional musical career that lay before him, and he now sought employment as a church organist. Doubtless he hoped that he, too, might become a Böhm, a Buxtehude or a Reincken; he may even have sensed that he possessed gifts that could take him still further.

Within the next few months, two posts became vacant. One was at the church of St Jacobi in Sangerhausen, and in the summer of 1702 Sebastian applied for it. He was interviewed and auditioned, and then accepted the post, but the reigning duke intervened in favour of an older and more experienced candidate of his own choice. The other was the position of organist at St George's Church in Eisenach, held, until his death early in 1703, by Johann Christoph Bach. However, it seems unlikely that, as an eighteen-year-old, Sebastian would have applied; at any rate, it went to yet another Bach, his cousin Johann Bernhard, nine years his senior.

For a while, therefore, Sebastian marked time, and we know that in March 1703 he was working as a violinist at the court of Duke Johann Ernst of Weimar and playing in a chamber orchestra. It seems that he also sometimes played the organ in the ducal chapel, since the court organist Johann Effler, a friend of the Bach family, was elderly and in fragile health. Sebastian must have been well thought of, since he also taught music to the duke's sons, the younger of whom learned to compose.

At this time, too, he benefited from getting to know the celebrated Weimar violinist Johann Paul von Westhoff, a pioneer in the technique of double-stopping and the first musician to compose unaccompanied works for the instrument. However, his sights remained set on obtaining a church post and finally, in August 1703, he became the organist of the Neukirche at Arnstadt, a town some thirty-five miles south east of Eisenach. He was now eighteen, and his childhood and formal musical apprenticeship were over.

CHAPTER 2

ARNSTADT AND MUHLHAUSEN
(1703–8)

- ♦ *Disgruntlement in Arnstadt*
- ♦ *A brilliant organist*
- ♦ *Promotion to Mühlhausen*
- ♦ *On to Weimar*

The Arnstadt appointment came about following the installation of a new organ. The instrument was ready by June 1703 and although an organist, Andreas Börner, was already nominally in place, the church authorities called on Bach to inaugurate it on 13 July and paid him a fee for doing so. Perhaps they already had it in mind to offer this exceptionally gifted young man the post of organist over Börner's head. At any rate, to avoid ill-feeling they assigned Börner to other work and asked Bach to accept the position. A month later he received his formal contract with the seal of the reigning Count Anton Günther.

This document tells us much about the social structure and manners of the time. It stated that Bach should 'cultivate the fear of God, sobriety and the love of peace, altogether avoiding bad company and any distraction from your calling, and generally conducting yourself in all things towards God, high authority and your superiors as befitting an honour-loving servant and organist.' In particular, he was enjoined to be 'faithful, gracious and obedient to his High Countly Grace'. In return for all this, and performing his musical duties with skill and diligence, he was to be paid an annual salary of fifty guilders and an allowance for board and lodging. This was higher than usual for a first post, and more than some of his relatives received even as experienced musicians. He was able to buy himself a harpsichord and acquire the first books of what was to become a respectable library. During his first year he seems to have lodged in an inn, the Golden Crown. This was also the residence of his second cousin, Maria Barbara Bach, and they soon became friends.

Bach's duties were reasonably light, involving two hours in church for the Sunday morning service, playing for further services on Mondays and Thursdays, and providing music for a prayer hour on Tuesdays. In general, he simply accompanied the hymns sung by the congregation and a choir, which he himself recruited, all male and consisting of boys and students. Thus he had ample free time, but we know little of how he spent it. He may have participated in the town's other musical activities, since these included court and theatre music. He may even have helped with the composition of a *Singspiel* (musical play) about beer-brewing, which took place in May 1705, perhaps with some of his choir taking part, for the local tax on beer helped to pay his salary. Its music, however, has been lost.

Indeed, up to this time there is little evidence of his work as a composer. It is certain that many student works have been lost, and it would be interesting to see them, for not even a genius such as Bach can become a master composer without learning his craft through supervised exercises and private experiments. However, from now on compositions survive with names and dates. (In 1950, 200 years after Bach's death, all of his known compositions were catalogued by the musicologist Wolfgang Schmieder. His *Bach Werke-Verzeichnis* (BWV) is now accepted as the standard means of numbering the composer's works.)

One is his *Capriccio on the Departure of a Beloved Brother* BWV992, a harpsichord piece probably written in 1703, when his brother Jakob, three years older than he, went to join a military band in Sweden. Unlike church music of the time, it is programmatic in content in a way that we associate more with later, Romantic composers. Thus, drooping chromatic phrases in the right hand, in the sombre key of F minor, are supposed to depict the sorrow of friends and relatives as Jakob takes his leave. The four movements, of which three are slow, are labelled with their meaning: the first portrays people trying to dissuade Jakob from his journey, the second shows their fears of what may befall him, the third is a lament, and the busy finale is the leavetaking itself, which includes the sounds of the departing stagecoach and a vigorous 'postilion's fugue'. In fact, Jakob travelled as far as Constantinople (now Istanbul), before dying in Stockholm in 1722 at the age of forty. He and Sebastian never met again.

This colourful Capriccio shows that Bach could imbue his music with a keen sense of mood. Although in later life he rarely used such a revealing title, his most characteristic music is expressive rather than abstract, and when he actually chose to tell a story, as in his great *St Matthew Passion*, the result is highly dramatic. In other words, he was not only a master of his craft, but also a man of flesh and blood, as an incident in the summer of 1705 showed.

A student called Johann Geyersbach, an unskilful bassoonist who played at the Neukirche, and was actually older than Bach himself, was rudely told by the young organist that he sounded like a goat. Not surprisingly, he took offence and on 4 August 1705, returning from a christening and doubtless slightly drunk, he took his revenge. On meeting Bach and Maria Barbara's elder sister in the street, he demanded an apology. Bach refused, and Geyersbach struck him with his stick, calling him a *Hundsfott*, or cur. Bach then drew a knife, but the others present separated the two. Bach complained to his church authorities, saying that he could not safely go about if Geyersbach were not punished and restrained, but they told him that he was himself partly responsible for the affray. Both young men were admonished.

Bach was already unhappy in Arnstadt and this incident did nothing to help matters. The church council had soon discovered that their brilliant young organist was also a touchy youth who had a mind of his own and was not afraid to express it forcefully. In October 1705, soon after the Geyersbach affair, he asked his cousin Johann Ernst Bach to deputize for him at the Neukirche and obtained a month's leave so that he could travel to Lübeck and hear Buxtehude play the magnificent organ at the Marienkirche. This was a journey of nearly three hundred miles, which he is said to have made partly on foot. The great Danish organist, then nearly seventy and approaching retirement, also directed concerts in the weeks leading up to Christmas, which Bach evidently attended. He may also have been present at a grand concert in memory of the Emperor Leopold I, who had died earlier in the year. It is just possible that he hoped to succeed Buxtehude in his post. However, a condition for this, which would have deterred him, was that the next organist should marry Buxtehude's daughter. She was ten years older than he and no beauty, and he may also by now have been contemplating marriage with Maria Barbara.

He remained in Lübeck until about the beginning of February 1706, having much overstayed his leave, and on returning to Arnstadt he had to make his excuses to the irate church authorities, who summoned him to Count Anton's palace on 21 February and demanded an explanation. They were even angrier when he defiantly justified his absence by saying he had been improving his musical skills in their interests and reproached him on other grounds, saying that he had failed to maintain good relations with his choir and should perform more concerted music with them, in other words the kind of church cantatas of which he later produced so many. He replied that he could play the organ for such occasions, but only if the church council provided a conductor. Yet another complaint was that he upset and confused churchgoers by making 'surprising variations' when playing hymns, indulging himself in improvisatory freedom instead of playing the plain accompaniments that his provincial congregation expected. Bach agreed to desist, and then deliberately stripped his playing down to an unmusical minimum. The church council knew that he was making fools of them, but could do little about it since he could claim that he was acting precisely as ordered. As a result, his relations with his employers were permanently soured.

This story says much about the young Bach. His musical ability could be heard and appreciated by all, but he was not a good subordinate and his sturdy independence of mind already marked him out before he was twenty. One of his modern biographers, Malcolm Boyd, writes of him at this time: 'As someone scarcely out of his teens, he must have appeared intolerably arrogant and self-willed, and, whatever posterity may think, the consistory had every right to question whether what Bach did for the Neukirche merited the salary they paid him.' Harsh, but probably fair, comment.

Later in 1706 he was once again in trouble with his employers for his poor control of his choristers, who sometimes played ball during church services, carried knives into school and frequented establishments of ill repute. As someone of much the same age as these youths, he had little chance of controlling them, but he was still held responsible. The church council also took him to task for inviting a 'stranger maiden' to his organ loft, but here he was able to show that he had obtained permission and that she had been singing to his accompaniment. She was almost certainly his future wife, Maria Barbara. The writing was on the wall, however, and he must have known that it was time for him to leave Arnstadt and seek a more congenial position. Even without his disagreements with his employers, it was clear that he had little hope of doing anything musically interesting or ambitious in Arnstadt.

His chance of a move came in December 1706 with the death of Johann Georg Ahle, the organist of St Blasius' Church, Mühlhausen. Lying some twenty miles north east of Eisenach, this imperial free city was governed by an elected council rather than a nobleman, and the church of St Blasius, one of its two principal churches, was an imposing building with a strong musical tradition. Its council already had in mind a successor to Ahle, but at the suggestion of a council member related to Bach by marriage, the young Johann Sebastian was invited to attend for a *Probe*, or audition, on 24 April 1707. On 14 June he was interviewed again and told the church council that he wished to receive the same salary as at Arnstadt. Although this was more than Ahle had earned, the council agreed and offered him the post. They also provided a wagon to move his belongings. Later that month, he resigned from his Arnstadt post, where he was succeeded by Johann Ernst Bach.

Bach was now twenty-two, and we can take further stock of the music that he had by now composed. His *Cantata No.4, 'Christ lag in Todes banden'*, may have been written for his *Probe* at Mühlhausen: based on a Lutheran chorale (hymn) melody as so many of his cantatas are, it is scored for solo voices and choir plus cornett, trombones, strings and a keyboard continuo (accompaniment) played on the organ. But because some of his early pieces were exercises based on the music of other composers, were unsigned and undated, or exist only in the form of copies made by others, uncertainties remain. One book on the composer describes his *Pastorale in F major*, BWV590, as among the best pieces of the Arnstadt years and an 'exquisite gem of sustained lyricism,' but immediately adds that its authenticity is 'under suspicion'. On the other hand, *Grove* lists it as authentic, but

assigns it to around 1710. Some scholars believe they have iden-
tified some twenty works of the Arnstadt period, but others are
more cautious. Among the earliest ones that are certainly by Bach
are the 'departure' *Capriccio* for his brother Jakob, the one-move-
ment *Harpsichord Capriccio in E major*, probably written in 1704,
which is inscribed 'in honour of' his Ohrdruf brother Johann
Christoph, and a lively keyboard *Sonata in D*, BWV963, with a
theme imitating hens and cuckoos. Three harpsichord *Toccatas*,
BWV913–915, alternate brilliant passagework and more stately
music: as to their date, *Grove* merely says 'before 1708'. Even so,
they are evidence of the future great composer experimenting.
Bach's nineteenth-century biographer Philipp Spitta thought the
E minor Toccata, the second of these, 'one of those pieces steeped
in melancholy which Bach alone could write', and it is worth
noticing that all three are in minor keys. However, it has been
suggested that the final section of this piece is a reworking of an
existing Italian one.

This is another reminder that Bach studied all the music that
came his way and caught his interest, whether it were German,
French or Italian. In later life, he was not ashamed to admit how
much he had learned from the music of others. After his death,
his son Carl Philipp Emanuel wrote of his father's early studies
of organ music by Reincken, Buxtehude, the German organist
Nicolaus Bruhns and the French one Nicolas de Grigny, informa-
tion that he must have been given by Johann Sebastian himself.

But for all Bach's wide-ranging interest in other musical
schools and styles, his roots were still in the music of the Lutheran
church services, in whose traditions he had been raised. In his
early twenties he also composed organ pieces based on chorale
melodies, such as his treatment of the hymn tunes, *'Wie schön
leuchtet der Morgenstern'*, BWV739, of which we have a manuscript
copy probably in his own hand, the earliest one known to exist.
There is also the Chorale Prelude *'Gelobet seist du, Jesu Christ'*,
BWV722, which intersperses simple statements of each phrase of
the tune with rich, improvisatory flourishes. Although we do not
know whether this was written at Arnstadt or in Mühlhausen, it
is likely that it was the elaborate kind of music, the 'sundry
embellishments' that, according to his Arnstadt employers, simply confused a congregation.

By now, Bach had also composed brilliant, original pieces for organ that showed off his finger dexterity and no less remarkable command of the pedal keyboard operated by the feet. These preludes and fugues include those listed as BWV531 and 533 and also BWV550 and 551. There are also fantasias, more free-ranging in shape as the name suggests, such as BWV563, 570 and 572.

But by far the best known piece belonging to these years is the *Toccata and Fugue in D minor*, BWV565. This is immensely dramatic music which raises splendid cathedrals of sound and seems to revel in mystery and mastery; timeless in its appeal, this music, arranged for a modern symphony orchestra, even inspired a memorable sequence in Walt Disney's 1940 film *Fantasia*. Probably written at around the time of Bach's twenty-first birthday in 1706, it shows unmistakably that this awkward young man had already earned his place in musical history. Of course he had inherited and profited from existing traditions of organ music, but this brilliant yet dignified *Toccata and Fugue* demonstrated that he was to enrich them still further.

MUHLHAUSEN

Bach arrived in Mühlhausen in the first few days of July 1707 and at once established himself as a composer as well as an organist. It may have been in this month that he composed his cantata, '*Aus der Tiefen rufe ich, Herr, zu dir*', a penitential work whose title is the biblical 'Out of the depths I cry unto thee, O Lord'. (Its number in the standard listing of Bach's cantatas is 131, but this bears no relation to its date of composition, and the same is true of *Cantata No.106*, mentioned below.) The sombre mood of this music for voices and orchestra, written for another Mühlhausen church (that of St Mary) and for a commemorative service following a serious fire in the city, hardly reflected his own probably hopeful state of mind but reminds us that, like any other church composer of his time, he was supposed to express pious community sentiments rather than exhibit his own soul. Similarly, when serving as a court musician, he wrote to satisfy his noble employer. As far as we know, he accepted this state of affairs throughout his life without complaint.

A month after he reached Mühlhausen, his maternal great-uncle Tobias Lämmerhirt died. He probably wrote his *Cantata No.106* for the funeral, which took place on 14 August; its title is '*Gottes Zeit ist die allerbeste Zeit*' ('God's Time is the Best'), although it is now sometimes also called the *Actus tragicus*. Here is music that powerfully sets the Old Testament message of mortality against the Christian reassurance of salvation, and sums all up with trust in God. Sombre though thoughts of death might be, Bach himself was surely a happy man, for his relative left him fifty guilders, more than half his annual salary of eighty-five guilders. This undoubtedly helped him to enter into his marriage to his second cousin Maria Barbara Bach. The wedding took place on 17 October at the village church in Dornheim, near Arnstadt, whose pastor Johann Lorenz Stauber was a friend of them both (a year later he married Maria Barbara's aunt). Six months older than Sebastian, Maria Barbara was also a musician, and two sons born to the young couple, Wilhelm Friedemann in 1710 and Carl Philipp Emanuel in 1714, were themselves to gain fame in their father's profession.

Bach's future now looked secure. But once again, and soon, he found himself less than happy in his job. Although his dealings with his Mühlhausen church council were amicable, he realized that his opportunities for writing concerted music for the Blasius-kirche were limited, for its pastor, Johann Adolf Frohne, inclined towards the German Pietist movement – which resembled English Puritanism – and liked church music to be simple. In practice, this meant that he wanted it mainly restricted to the plain singing of hymns and liturgical texts. Bach quickly became frustrated, and his temperament did not take kindly to the situation. Further-more, Pastor Frohne was on poor personal terms with the pastor of the Marienkirche, Georg Christian Eilmar, for whom Bach had composed *Cantata No.131*, and who believed that elaborate music had its role in church services.

Indeed, the founder of Lutheranism, Martin Luther, had himself been a musician, and had stated, 'Music is a beautiful and lovely gift of God and a queen over every movement of the human heart; nothing on earth is more powerful than noble music.' This was certainly also Bach's belief, but Pastor Frohne seems to have considered that anything beyond the simplest church music smacked of vanity and therefore should be shunned. According to Bach's biographer Jan Chiapusso, Frohne 'was guilty of thwarting the genius in his endeavours of art and religious conscience . . . the church and its pastor refused Bach's every attempt to use his great musical gifts for their services of worship.' This is probably too unkind to Frohne, who was no more conservative than many clergy of his time and may have seen Bach less as a genius than as an opinionated youth who failed in loyalty to his own church. At any rate, he and his organist could not see eye to eye, and matters were not helped when Bach composed for the rival Marienkirche. Nor was Frohne happy when Pastor Eilmar became a friend of the young couple and later, in December 1708, the godfather of their first child, Catharina Dorothea.

Eilmar provided the texts for Bach's *Cantata No.71, 'Gott ist mein König'*. This was a brilliant celebratory piece composed for a semi-secular occasion, the inauguration of Mühlhausen's new city council on 4 February 1708. The day was festive throughout, with a procession of forty-eight robed dignitaries from the city hall to the Marienkirche, where the cantata was performed by solo voices, a choir and an orchestra that included three trumpets and drums as well as the usual wind, strings and organ. The whole day ended with a banquet and the consumption of a huge cake made by local bakers. As for the new cantata, the city council liked it so much that they had it printed.

But all was not so well at the Blasiuskirche. Apart from his uneasy relations with Pastor Frohne, Bach was dissatisfied with the organ and told the church council in February 1708 that it needed repairs and additions. In the same month he drew up a specification of his requirements, which they considered and accepted. Yet this was not enough to content him; he may already have been thinking of moving on again, and four months later he resigned. Before doing so, he did two things. One was to write another *Church Cantata* (No.196) for the wedding on 5 June of Pastor Stauber to Maria Barbara's aunt Regina Wedemann, and the other was to audition successfully as an organist for the court of Duke Wilhelm Ernst of Weimar.

He was thus now ready to leave Mühlhausen, and from the letter of resignation that he wrote to his church council on 25 June it is clear that, at twenty-five, neither his ambition nor his prickly temperament had been subdued. Indeed, his resignation letter, in which he proudly mentioned his invitation to the Weimar court, was bluntly critical. He complained that at the Blasiuskirche he had been prevented from honouring God with proper music; that he had suffered hindrance and vexation; that performances in nearby villages in which he had sometimes taken part often surpassed that of his own church; that he had maintained the organ in the face of opposition; that he had spent his own money on music for the church's library, and finally that his salary was insufficient despite his simple lifestyle. At Weimar, he declared, he would at last be able 'to pursue the ultimate aim of properly conceived church music'.

It says something for the church council that they did not dismiss the letter as arrogant. Instead, they tried to persuade Bach to withdraw it and only accepted it with reluctance 'since he could not be made to stay'. They seem to have recognized the justice of Bach's strictures, and in return he offered them his services in continuing to supervise the rebuilding and repair work on the Blasiuskirche organ. A year later, the council paid him to return to Mühlhausen to take part in a Reformation festival. He must have composed music for this and another such festival in 1710, but it has been lost. He also probably inaugurated the rebuilt organ when it was completed in 1709, and may have composed his famous organ chorale '*Ein' feste Burg ist unser Gott*' BWV720 (a tune adapted by Luther himself) for the occasion.

He was succeeded at the Blasiuskirche by his cousin Johann Friedrich Bach, slightly older than himself and the third son of his Eisenstadt uncle Johann Christoph Bach. It must have seemed to people in the region that the Bach family were everywhere, musically-speaking. J.F. Bach's appointment proved much longer-lasting, for he remained at Mühlhausen until his death in 1730.

Although Bach's point in his resignation letter, that moving to Weimar would allow him to pursue his higher aims for church music, is an indication of his musical ideals, it was hardly the whole story, for his salary at Weimar was to be 150 guilders a year, nearly twice what he received at Mühlhausen. In 1711 it was to rise again by fifty guilders and three years later, when he was appointed *Konzertmeister* to the Weimar court, it became 250 guilders, five times what he had earned on beginning work at Arnstadt a decade earlier. In fact, Bach knew that by going to Weimar he was bettering himself and accepting a post of prestige. He also knew fairly accurately what musical prospects the new appointment would offer. In his own words to his church council, he was receiving 'the most gracious admission of His Serene Highness of Saxe-Weimar into his Court *Kapelle* and Chamber Music'.

The word *Kapelle* means chapel, but in those days it commonly meant an instrumental or vocal ensemble, so that Bach's description of his new job might seem unconnected with church music. But he knew that he could expect to play the organ for religious services in the ducal chapel, a place of importance to the devout Duke Wilhelm Ernst. The most powerful figure in Weimar, he had ruled for some years with his younger brother Duke Johann Ernst, in accordance with a family law established in the previous century. However, the music-loving Johann Ernst had died fairly young, in 1707, leaving the court in the care of the serious-minded Wilhelm, childless and a divorcee. He, too, appreciated music and it was he who had offered Bach his new post after hearing him play. There was a younger generation at court in the persons of Johann Ernst's two sons, of whom the elder, Ernst August, was to attain his majority in 1709; but although he then became co-regent, his uncle effectively remained in charge.

During Bach's stay at Weimar five years before, he had struck up a friendship with the court's elderly organist Johann Effler and had almost certainly sometimes deputized for him. Now, Effler needed the help of a younger man all the more and, indeed, on being appointed on 14 July 1708, Bach received the title of *Hoforganist* (court organist). Effler may have had a hand in this, for he knew that he could not continue much longer. In December 1709, an 'old, sick servant', he retired and died just two years later. Bach therefore expected to become a central figure of the Weimar court, both as an organist and as a chamber musician (*Cammermusikus*) who played the harpsichord, violin or viola in an orchestra. As far as we know, his expectations were justified and his new appointment proved congenial to him. He and Maria Barbara were to remain at Weimar until 1717, and six of their children were born there, beginning with Catharina Dorothea in December 1708.

CHAPTER 3
WEIMAR AND COTHEN
(1709–28)

♦ *Characteristic stubbornness*
♦ *Prince Leopold of Cöthen's Kapellmeister*
♦ *Death of his wife*

Since Bach had been brought up as a devout Lutheran who saw his art as serving God, it may seem that now, aged twenty-five, he had become worldly in leaving his career as a church organist to serve a secular ruler. At that time, however, such a ruler was seen as God's representative, governing men's worldly affairs just as the church attended to their immortal souls. Every court had its chapel and strict religious observances. In Weimar's case this was especially so, for Duke Wilhelm Ernst had studied theology and sometimes questioned his servants about the sermons they heard at Sunday services, where attendance was compulsory. Nevertheless, things were done in the grand manner, as befitted a leading ducal court, and Bach knew that he need fear no austerity or penny-pinching. There was even an elderly resident poet, Johann Christoph Lorbeer, whose works, much approved of by the duke for their moral tone, included *Lob der edlen Musik* (The Praise of Noble Music), while another man of letters, the court librarian Salomo Franck, was to collaborate with Bach in the composition of church cantatas.

Thus Weimar's court musicians had their importance, although they were still servants and strictly governed in many matters, such as their dress (Bach must have worn livery). As for the music that Bach composed here, it was supposed to have qualities of harmony, dignity and propriety, reflecting the properly governed state which Weimar was considered to be. As his biographer Hannsdieter Wohlfarth has put it, 'God's creation was still understood as a well-ordered community', and he quotes the philosopher Leibniz, a contemporary of Bach and a courtier himself: 'Because the universe as a whole is fully ordered by God, so complete order must rule in each individual being.' The intellectual climate was such that people were not expected to question the existing social order, and although new ideals of human brotherhood, freedom and equality were now awakening in Europe, no one in this part of Germany could voice them without risking his career and perhaps his liberty.

Bach, however, was no revolutionary, and from his point of view the life of the Weimar court was rich. Duke Wilhelm had reinstated its *Kapelle*, a flexible body of musicians with a dozen or so instruments, including string players and trumpeters, sometimes supplemented by military bandsmen, and several singers, including choirboys. Some of these musicians were versatile and could take on more than one role: for example, one of the tenors, Johann Döbernitz, also played the bassoon. The *Kapellmeister*, or overall director of music, was Johann Samuel Drese, who had been at the court for some years. He was assisted by his son Johann Wilhelm, an arrangement which, while sounding unsatisfactorily nepotistic, worked well enough. However, neither Drese possessed outstanding gifts, and the father was now well into his sixties, so that Johann Wilhelm seems to have taken on some of his duties. As in the case of the organist Effler, here was a situation where Bach could bide his time and hope for promotion; and probably his noble employer thought on similar lines.

Bach's duties do not seem to have been onerous. He played the organ in the Himmelsburg, as the ducal chapel was called, and took part in chamber music, but this still left time for other things. A pupil from Mühlhausen, Johann Martin Schubart, came to Weimar to study with him and was later to succeed him as court organist. In due course he also acquired other pupils; amongst whom were Johann Caspar Vogler (who in turn succeeded Schubart) and Johann Tobias Krebs. He also now taught two young relatives, Johann Lorenz Bach and his Ohrdruf nephew Johann Bernhard Bach, the latter then being a boy who would eventually succeed his father Johann Christoph Bach as organist of the Michaeliskirche in Ohrdruf.

Bach continued to pursue his interest in organ-building, an

area of knowledge in which his skill was now widely valued. He was also paid in 1709, and again in 1710, for repairing harpsichords belonging to the sons of the late Duke Johann Ernst. At this time, when a great deal of organ building and rebuilding was being undertaken in Germany, he was often consulted and seems to have freely given advice and encouragement. When an organ builder called Nicolaus Trebs, whom he had known at Mühl-hausen, was invited to construct a new instrument at Taubach, a village near Weimar, he asked Bach to make out its specification and test it on its completion in 1710. In his turn, Bach liked Trebs and in a testimonial written the following year, called him 'a reasonable and conscientious man' – sober eighteenth-century words that nevertheless implied high praise. He then invited Trebs to work on the Weimar organ in the Himmelsburg, which with its two manuals and twenty-five stops was a small instrument compared to some that Bach had heard and played in Hamburg and Lübeck; it was also smaller than the one at the Blasiuskirche in Mühlhausen. Between 1712 and 1714, and under Bach's supervision, Trebs set about making improvements and additions and seems to have given satisfaction. In November 1713, Bach invited Trebs to be a godfather to his son Johann Gottfried.

Another friend was the organist of Weimar's Stadtkirche, Johann Gottfried Walther. He and Bach were related through a maternal grandfather, and when he and his wife had a son in 1712, Bach agreed to be a godfather. They shared an interest in Italian music and Walther introduced Bach to works by such contemporary masters of the concerto form as Corelli and Vivaldi, whose music Bach then sometimes arranged for organ. It seems that Walther once challenged Bach's boast that he could play any organ music at sight by presenting him with something virtually impossible which defeated him. Their relationship did not suffer, as was once thought, but the story is significant because there is little doubt that even Bach's friends sometimes wanted to dent his high opinion of his own remarkable gifts.

It is not known where Bach and his growing family lived during these Weimar years, except that he does not seem to have stayed in the castle itself. This was actually a distinction, since most of those in the duke's employ were required to do so. Even the *Kapellmeister*, Drese, lived there and was allowed to draw from the kitchen a daily loaf of bread and measure of beer. However, we know that in March 1709 Bach and his wife, together with a sister of hers, were lodging with the court singer and 'master of the pages', Adam Immanuel Weldig. It is likely that they stayed there until the summer of 1713, when Weldig left Weimar to take up another post. But they kept in touch, and Weldig was to be a godfather of Carl Philipp Emanuel Bach, born on 8 March 1714. This boy was destined to be the most famous Bach after his father, a man admired by both Haydn and Mozart for opening up the way to new forms and feelings in music. Another of his godfathers was the distinguished musician Georg Philipp Telemann, a former *Kapellmeister* at Eisenach.

Although Bach seems to have been content enough at Weimar, in the last months of 1713, after five years there, he once again considered a move. He visited the university town of Halle, Handel's birthplace, and heard of the death of the Liebfrauenkirche organist Friedrich Wilhelm Zachow, Handel's teacher. The instrument that Zachow had played was about to be enlarged, and Bach was tempted. It seems that the pastor, Johann Michael Heineccius, pressed Bach to apply for the post and that he did so, composing a cantata in support of his application which may have been his No.63, '*Christen, ätzet diesen Tag*', possibly with a text by Heineccius.

On 14 December he was offered a contract, but by then he was having second thoughts, not least because the basic salary of 171 thalers was less than he earned at Weimar. A month later he wrote back to Halle enquiring closely as to the additional perquisites of wedding fees and the like (the *Accidentien*) which traditionally added to an organist's salary, as they often do today. His prospective employers replied that while these should be substantial, they could make no guarantees, and asked him to make up his mind. It is almost certain that he then went to Duke Wilhelm, for on 2 March 1714, 'at his most humble request', he was promoted to *Konzertmeister*, ranking below the Vice-*Kapellmeister* J.W. Drese but now third among Weimar's court musicians, at an annual salary of 250 florins. (There were several currencies in Germany at this time, but the guilder, thaler and florin seem to have had roughly the same value.) After this, he formally refused the Halle post.

Not surprisingly, some people felt that Bach had used Halle

as a lever to improve his position at Weimar, and he found himself on rather shaky ground morally, if not legally. The Liebfrauen-kirche council instructed their lawyer August Becker to pursue the matter. But in a letter to Becker dated 19 March 1714, Bach denied that he had actively sought the post at Halle ('as I see it, I allowed my name to go forward'), and added sharply that 'no one can be expected to move to a place where he will be worse off ... it should not be concluded from all this that I have deceived the worshipful Collegium so as to persuade my gracious master to increase my salary; he already holds my service and my art in such regard that there is no need for me to travel to Halle in order to improve my salary here. I am sorry then, that what the worshipful Collegium was so certain of has turned out so uncer-tainly.' Fortunately, this explanation was accepted and he made his peace with Halle. In April 1716 he and two other well-known organists were invited to the Liebfrauenkirche to examine and inaugurate the new organ there, receiving a substantial fee and expenses for the days that they spent in the city.

Bach soon knew that he had made the right decision in staying at Weimar, for in March 1715 Duke Wilhelm ordered that his *Konzertmeister* should receive a share of the perquisites and honoraria earned by the *Kapelle*. In effect, he was being recognised as a deputy *Kapellmeister*. Furthermore, his salary now exceeded that of *Kapellmeister* Drese, perhaps because he now composed a cantata each month for performance in the Himmelsburg. The first of these cantatas was No.182 (as usual, the numbers bear no relation to dates of composition), '*Himmelskönig, sei willkommen*', and it was first performed on Palm Sunday 1714, not long after he took up his new appointment.

However, of the works Bach composed while at Weimar, the most important are those that he wrote for the organ. Thirty-nine major organ pieces date from these years, 1708–17, more than he wrote in the three decades that remained to him after he left the city. They include his noble *Passacaglia in C minor*, BWV582, and numerous preludes, toccatas, fantasias and fugues. Here, it is has been said, are works that 'stand as eternal monuments, profoundly expressive of deep, ecstatic spiritual experience ... while still burning with his ardent fire of youth.' There are also pieces based on chorale melodies, including several that make up a set called the *Orgel-Büchlein* or 'Little Organ Book', BWV599–644, wittily inscribed as for 'a beginner at the organ' and also 'in praise of the Almighty's will, and for my neighbour's greater skill'. The words may seem curious, but were probably not false modesty, for Bach never stopped learning and, encouraged by his colleague Walther, studied Italian organ music by such men as Frescobaldi, Albinoni, and Bonporti and made copies of it for himself. He wrote other keyboard pieces for the harpsichord, including his six *English Suites*, BWV806–11, and numerous arrangements of violin concertos by Vivaldi, the Italian composer most admired by the young Duke Johann Ernst, who then played them for himself. Bach also made two-handed arrangements of two concertos by Johann Ernst himself and one of a violin concerto by Telemann.

Among the cantatas from Bach's Weimar years is the secular *'Hunt' Cantata*, *'Was mir behagt, ist nur die muntre Jagd'*, BWV208, a delightfully vigorous piece composed for the birthday of Duke Christian of Saxe-Weissenfels in 1713, which includes the tactfully loyal sentiment, 'Where the sovereign ruleth wisely, joy and peace the land have blessed.' This had words by Salomo Franck, as did the *Church Cantatas Nos.12, 31, 132, 152, 155, 161, 162, 165, 185* and almost certainly others. Together these two men made the Lutheran church cantata into something shapely and colourful, even dramatic, with operatic devices such as recitatives and arias married to specially written texts that paraphrased biblical ones or otherwise expressed pious sentiments. In later life, writing cantatas with another poet, Picander, Bach recommended Franck to him as a model of style.

However, Bach's production of cantatas fluctuated after the beginning of 1716, with none at all dating from most of that year and then three coming in quick succession at its end, all of which are lost in their original form, although we have revisions of them that Bach made in 1723. This may have been because he seems at this time to have given his services increasingly to the young co-regent, Duke Ernst August, who occupied a part of the Wilhelmsburg called the Rotes Schloß, or Red Castle. Ernst August's brother Johann Ernst had also lived there until chronic illness made him leave Weimar in 1714 (he died in the following year), and, as we have seen, Bach had shared his passion for the Italian music that he brought back from his studies at Utrecht University in 1711–13. With his untimely death so soon after this, Bach must have felt a keen sense of loss and, as a result, was all the more loyal to his brother Ernst August. Unfortunately, there was some ill-feeling between the young duke and his gloomy uncle Wilhelm, and at one stage Wilhelm even imposed fines on members of his household who provided services for his nephew. Bach seems to have defied the disapproval of his employer and joined in a presentation to Ernst August on the occasion of his marriage to a sister of Prince Leopold of Anhalt-Cöthen in January 1716, and he also gave another performance of his '*Hunt*' *Cantata* for the young duke's birthday three months later.

Because of this, and perhaps for other reasons of which we know nothing, relations between Bach and his employer deteriorated, matters coming to a head when *Kapellmeister* Drese died in December 1716. Since his son was not greatly gifted, Bach hoped strongly for promotion as the aged Drese's successor, and his composition of three cantatas in the month of Drese's death may have represented his vigorous bid for the appointment. Instead, Duke Wilhelm snubbed him not once but twice, first by inviting Telemann to accept the post and then, when Telemann declined, by offering it to the younger Drese, who naturally accepted at once.

Duke Wilhelm had thus made it crystal clear to Bach that his prospects of promotion at Weimar were closed, and once again he started to look for another post. But now he wanted nothing less than the position of *Kapellmeister*, and very soon he found the prospect of one at the court of Prince Leopold of Anhalt-Cöthen, Duke Ernst August's brother-in-law. Leopold may have been present at his sister's recent Weimar wedding, to which Bach had contributed music; alternatively, she may have given good reports of him. Whatever the case, the existing leader of the Cöthen *Kapelle*, Augustin Retinae Stricker, was reaching the end of his three-year contract, and by the beginning of August the Prince had invited Bach to replace him at a salary of 400 thalers, about a third more than he was paid at Weimar. He even started paying Bach's salary at once.

But he and Bach had both reckoned without Duke Wilhelm. Perhaps suspecting his nephew's hand in all this, he flatly refused to let Bach go and attempted to sweeten the pill by allowing him to travel to Dresden, probably in September, and then setting up an endowment fund for all his court musicians to mark his birthday on 30 October. Bach remained unimpressed, but was still at Weimar when the birthday and the bicentenary of the Reformation were marked by three days of festivities. They must have included music, yet as far as we know he composed no cantata for the occasion, and this may have seemed like insubordination to his employer, who was, after all, a near-absolute ruler who expected to have his way.

However, Duke Wilhelm, like others before him, was up against Bach's characteristic stubbornness. For a while there was a stalemate, during which he might have realized that he could gain nothing by keeping his employee against his will. But Bach became impatient, and evidently demanded his release so forcefully that Wilhelm had him confined to his quarters from 6 November (some accounts even use the word 'imprisoned'). Whether this was supposed to make Bach give in or simply intended as a humiliation, it made no difference: he was determined to leave and eventually Duke Wilhelm admitted defeat. But it was in disgrace and without ceremony that Bach and his family left Weimar for Cöthen on 2 December 1717.

COTHEN

Although Bach was exchanging one court for another, Cöthen had a very different ruler. Prince Leopold was a young man, born nine years after Bach in 1694. Like Bach, he had suffered the childhood loss of his father; he also showed musical talent, and at thirteen persuaded his widowed mother to employ court musicians with whom he could perform. Before he was twenty he had travelled widely, visiting England among other countries, and had become a skilled player of stringed instruments and the harpsichord. He also developed a good bass voice. On reaching his majority in 1715, he formed a *Kapelle* of his own at Cöthen, calling it his *collegium musicum*. By 1716 it amounted to eighteen instrumentalists, playing strings, wind and keyboard.

Cöthen (now spelt Köthen), situated to the north of Halle, was, and remains, a smallish town, and Bach must have found the court atmosphere more congenial than the chilly grandeur of Duke Wilhelm's court at Weimar. Prince Leopold's palace was in the town centre but, surrounded by a moat and well-tended gardens, it was an island of privileged comfort and culture set apart from the commoners' world. As at Weimar, Bach and his family seem to have lodged outside the castle, but it is not known where. Tradition has placed them in the Wallstraße, but it now seems more likely that they lived first at 11 Stiftstraße and then at 12 Holzmarkt.

Bach arrived in Cöthen in the first week of December 1717, in time to join in celebrations for the Prince's birthday and may have hastily written a cantata or other new piece, since the court accounts suggest that something was performed. Leopold evidently gave his new *Kapellmeister* some freedom, for only a week after this, he travelled to Leipzig to test an organ newly built by Johann Scheibe for the Paulinuskirche, the university church; however, this is the only work of that kind that he seems to have done during his six years at Cöthen.

It was at Cöthen that Maria Barbara Bach gave birth to the last of her seven children, a son born on 17 November 1718. He was named Leopold Augustus, and it was a mark of the Prince's regard for Bach that he agreed to be a godfather to the child who took his name and that the christening took place in the court chapel. Sadly, the boy was to die before his first birthday.

Although Bach had left Weimar from time to time on business, he travelled still more from Cöthen, and further afield. This was partly because the prince himself was often on the move: in May and June of 1718, for example, Bach and five of his musicians attended Leopold during his annual summer sojourn at the popular spa town of Carlsbad, some considerable distance to the south. Early in 1719 Bach went alone on another long trip, this time north to Berlin to purchase a new harpsichord for his *Kapelle*. (It may have been here or in Carlsbad that he met the Margrave Christian Ludwig of Brandenburg, to whom he was later to dedicate his *Brandenburg Concertos*.) It was for this instrument, a large two-manual one by a Berlin maker called Michael Mietke, that he wrote the important solo part in the *Fifth Brandenburg Concerto*, completed two years later, and almost certainly he played it at the first performance of the work, which took place at Cöthen.

In the same year Bach made the first of two unsuccessful efforts to meet his great contemporary Handel, now resident in England. Born in the same year, they had gone different ways, for while Bach had travelled relatively little, Handel was already a cosmopolitan and equally at home in Italian opera and English odes. Like every musician, Bach knew of his outstanding gifts –

he was, for example, equally at home in Italian opera and English odes – and, on hearing that he was visiting Halle, his birthplace just twenty miles away, set off by coach to visit him. He arrived only to find that Handel had left earlier the same day. Ten years later, something similar was to happen: Handel came again to Halle, but Bach, now in Leipzig and unwell, sent his son Wilhelm Friedemann to ask his colleague to visit him. Unfortunately, Handel was unable to do so, and Bach was grieved never to have met 'this truly great man of whom he thought so highly'.

Apart from this disappointment, these early years at Cöthen were happy ones. Still in his thirties, Bach held the highest musical rank then available as a *Kapellmeister*, for he was answerable only to his employer and wholly in charge of court music. His salary equalled that of the court's highest officers. His duties seem to have been light, consisting mainly of performing with his small orchestra (*Kapelle*) and composing music for this or that courtly occasion. The only drawback was that the court organ was a small, two-manual one with just thirteen stops, but that does not seem to have worried him too much, although he now composed little organ music. As at Weimar, he also had pupils, among them perhaps the prince himself. All in all, these were conditions that favoured creativity and contentment, and perhaps for the first time he found himself at ease both with his employer and with the musicians who played and sang under his direction. His own description of Cöthen in later life sums it up: 'There I had a gracious prince, who both loved and knew music, and in his service I intended to spend the rest of my life.'

However, his circumstances were soon to change, for in 1720 he lost his wife and in the following year Prince Leopold married a lady who had no interest in music. In May 1720, Leopold went again to take the waters at Carlsbad and took Bach with him. But this time he stayed longer than the five weeks or so of earlier visits, and was still there in July. In the meantime, Maria Barbara Bach died and was buried on 7 July. The cause of her death is not recorded: it may have been in childbirth, though a sudden summer fever seems more likely, since their son Carl Philipp Emanuel later wrote of his mother's 'illness'. No news of her death reached Bach in Carlsbad. It is possible that the Cöthen officials failed to send word to him, but more likely that the Prince and his staff were leaving for home at about the same time. Thus, having left his wife in good health, Bach returned to find her buried. As Carl Philipp Emanuel Bach later wrote, 'The news that she had been ill and died reached him only when he entered his own house.' She was only thirty-five.

Bach's biographer Malcolm Boyd has suggested that this was such a blow to him that 'life at Cöthen, which until then had been the happiest he had known, must now have become distasteful.' But that seems too black-and-white a way of looking at it. After all, like everyone of his time, he was familiar with premature death, for he and his wife had lost four of their seven children. His thirteen years of marriage to Maria Barbara had been 'blissful', according to the later testimony of their son Carl Philipp Emanuel, but although he mourned, he was too rational and active a man to give in to self-pitying, protracted grief.

Even so, his wife's death did unsettle him, and may have made him think that, after a dozen years of court service in Weimar and Cöthen, he ought now to return to the kind of church post for which his Lutheran schooling had fitted him so well and which he had sought at the start of his career. Two months after his bereavement, he may have applied for a vacant organist's post at the Jacobikirche in Hamburg, where there was a fine, relatively new four-manual organ with sixty stops. Although no correspondence exists proving an application, he did visit Hamburg and by 21 November his name was one of eight being considered by the church council, which could only have happened with his consent. One attraction the post had for him was that the pastor of the Jakobikirche, Erdmann Neumeister, was a friend and had written some of his cantata texts; another may have been that it offered educational and other facilities for his three motherless sons, and he may have remembered his own upbringing in a church school and all it had given him.

Although he did not attend the official auditions planned by the Jakobikirche council, returning to Cöthen just before they began on 28 November, he seems to have been heard, for during his visit to Hamburg he played the Jacobikirche organ and two others by the same maker, Arp Schnitger, that were in the Nikolaikirche and Johanniskirche. What appears to have been his formal audition took place in the Catharinenkirche, where he played for over two hours before city officials and an interested public. However, the listener who meant most to him was the church's own organist, J.A. Reincken, whom he had heard there as a Lüneburg schoolboy. Reincken had held this post for over sixty years and was now an unbelievable ninety-seven. Bach had heard him improvise, on this same organ, on the chorale melody '*By the Waters of Babylon*', and now someone asked Bach to take the same melody as the basis for an extemporization. After he had played for nearly half an hour, using a succession of styles to cumulative effect, the aged Reincken was deeply moved, saying, 'I thought that this art had perished, but I see that it still lives in you.'

Bach was strongly placed for the Jacobikirche post, for three other candidates did not attend for auditions and the remaining four did not meet the council's expectations. It was formally offered to him, and by 12 December the church council was awaiting his reply. However, he now refused it and the post was given instead to a little-known organist called Johann Joachim Heitmann, an appointment that had as much to do with the age-old practice of simony (the sale of church appointments) as with artistic talent. The Jacobikirche council had actually stated that, at the time of appointment, while musical ability was the chief consideration, the chosen candidate might 'of his own free will give a token of his gratitude' which the church could accept and use as needed. When it became known that Heitmann, on being appointed, had presented the church with a substantial sum (4,000 marks), someone described him scornfully as using cash better than his fingers, while Pastor Neumeister thundered that 'if an angel from Bethlehem came from heaven and played divinely but had no money, he would have to fly away again'. Bach must have known of this unsavoury aspect of the appointment, and it may have made him abandon the idea of moving. It has also been suggested that he had hoped, if appointed, to become the overall director of music in this great Hanseatic city, but realized that this would not happen. Although the matter of the Jacobikirche came to nothing, Bach's scrupulous honesty and directness would not have let him conceal his plans from his employer, and it says something for this kindly young nobleman that he was prepared, however reluctantly, to let his treasured *Kapellmeister* go. He must, however, have been glad when Bach abandoned the idea of the Hamburg post.

Thus, at the end of 1720, it seemed that Bach would remain

at Cöthen for the foreseeable future, with congenial work and a sympathetic employer. Yet he must have found life difficult as a widower with three young sons to care for; the boys were now aged ten (Wilhelm Friedemann), six (Carl Philipp Emanuel) and five (Johann Gottfried Bernhard). However, nothing is known of how he coped domestically, since his first biographers, writing well after his death and mainly interested in his music, recorded little about his personal affairs.

This was the time of the completion of the six *Brandenburg Concertos*, BWV1046–51, dedicated to the Margrave of Brandenburg in fulsome French and dated 24 March 1721. English biographers usually quote Bach as saying that he 'took a couple of years' over their composition, but the German phrase *ein paar Jahre* means 'a few years' or even 'some years', and he actually composed them over a period of about a decade, with Nos.3 & 6 being written in Weimar and the latter possibly dating back to 1708. The others probably date from his four Cöthen years, with No.5, the last to be composed, being written for the Mietke harpsichord that he had acquired in Berlin. The odd thing about this apparent commission from a nobleman, however, is that, as far as is known, Bach received no fee, nor even a letter of thanks. Indeed, the margrave seems to have accepted the music very casually. Perhaps he knew that these pieces, fine though they were, had not been composed especially for him or his court, which in fact did not have the musicians to perform them. When he died and some of his effects were disposed of, the manuscripts of these concertos were seen not to have been used. But Bach undoubtedly performed them at Cöthen, joining his musicians in bringing them to life.

These *Brandenburg Concertos* are joyful works, which sum up the orchestral side of Bach's art at this stage of his career, when he was in his mid-thirties and at the height of his powers. They are not concertos in the modern sense of works for a single soloist in dialogue, or conflict, with a full symphony orchestra, but works for smaller groups of instruments with individual or group solos as needed; another, more accurate, term for such music is *concerto grosso*. Thus, although the harpsichord is prominent in No.5 and the trumpet features strongly in No.2, they are not the only soloists in these pieces, and No.3 is for three violas, three violas da gamba and three cellos (plus keyboard continuo) and has no soloist at all, although the groups exchange ideas with each other. Nor is the number of movements fixed: No.1 has four movements, No.2 three, and No.3 just two, linked by a single bar of two slow chords. These works embody Bach's flexible views as to musical form and also the fact that in his time the word 'concerto' often simply meant music for several instruments playing as an ensemble. His own title for the pieces was *Concerts avec plusieurs instruments*.

Two other orchestral works from the Cöthen years are the first and last of four *Suites*, BWV1066–69. Again these are in several movements but are more expansive than the concertos. All four offer ceremonial yet genial music; however, the *Third Suite*, with its famous slow melody that later acquired the name *Air on the G string* (Bach's title is merely *Air*), was written, like the *Second*, after the composer left Cöthen for Leipzig.

It was also at Cöthen that Bach wrote most of his chamber music, that is, music for just three or four players rather than a bigger ensemble. There are two trio sonatas, one for two flutes and harpsichord and the other for violin, oboe and harpsichord, plus six sonatas for violin and harpsichord and others for flute. In addition, he composed six sonatas and partitas, BWV1001–6, for unaccompanied violin. The difference between the two forms resembles that between concertos and suites: sonatas and concertos are more formal and alternate slow and fast movements, while a partita or suite has a sequence of dance movements. At the time when Bach was composing, the dances normally used were the allemande, courante, sarabande and gigue, and they all feature in his six suites for unaccompanied violin, BWV1007–12. However, in Bach's hands the form was flexible and he added other dances to these suites, namely minuets in Nos.1 & 2, bourrées in Nos.2 & 3, and gavottes in Nos.3 & 4. As a practical man, he must have had a player in mind when composing such pieces as these, where the artistic and technical difficulties are of a high order, but we do not know who he was.

He also composed keyboard music, some of it for his son and pupil Wilhelm Friedemann. It was for him that he composed, section by section, what he called a *Clavier-Büchlein für Wilhelm Friedemann Bach*, which begins with an explanation of notation and ornaments and goes on to practise basic fingerwork. The *Two-part and Three-part Inventions*, BWV772–86 and 787–801, fifteen of each, also belong in this collection: each is in a single movement and the names refer to the number of contrapuntal parts or 'voices' involved. Wilhelm Friedemann ('Friede', as his father affectionately called him) must have made rapid progress, something which his teacher probably took for granted, for the collection came to include some of the preludes in what was to be one of Bach's greatest keyboard works, the first book of the *Well-Tempered Clavier* (or *Forty-Eight Preludes and Fugues*), BWV846–69, which dates from 1722 and uses all the major and minor keys in turn. Bach seems to have been a patient and methodical teacher who liked his work, at least with intelligent and diligent pupils. He did not force them (there were others too at this time), but gently guided them through the basics of notation and keyboard work. In the foreword to the *Two-part and Three-part Inventions*, he wrote that here was 'a clear way' to play in two and three parts and 'to attain a singing style in playing and also to gain a strong sense of composition'. Technique was never an end in itself, but always had to serve music.

In 1722, Bach was to begin another *Büchlein*, this time for a new member of the family, for on 3 December 1721, almost exactly two years after his wife's death, he remarried. Anna Magdalena Wilcke was just twenty, the daughter of a musician and briefly a *Sängerin* (singer) at the nearby court of Anhalt-Zerbst; she must have played an instrument too, since she was described as a *Musicantin* (musician). Bach knew the court and may have met her there, and she may have sung at Cöthen as a visitor. It seems that he then brought her to Cöthen on a more permanent basis, for she was described as 'a court singer here' when, on 25 September, both she and Bach became godparents to the son of Prince Leopold's butler Christian Hahn. Bach did not insist on her giving up her Cöthen post when they married, for he valued her skills and her salary was useful. She, in turn, may have enjoyed being able to continue in her profession, and helped her husband by proving to be a neat and accurate copyist of his music. Prince Leopold must have welcomed the marriage since it would help to keep his *Kapellmeister* at Cöthen, and he gave Bach permission to marry in his own home. To help the celebrations, the happy bridegroom visited the town's cellars to buy Rhine wine at a discount price of twenty per cent.

Soon after the marriage, Bach began providing Anna Magdalena with keyboard pieces, some of which are agreeably light in style while others are more challenging. She seems to have been a good woman and a good companion, and Bach knew that if he should die she would be a mother to her stepchildren (she herself was to give him thirteen more children). He even wrote lines to this effect alongside some of the music that he composed for her, as well as a short love poem ending:

> *O how with joy my heart is filled*
> *To see your beauty blooming,*
> *Till all my soul with music's thrilled,*
> *My heart's with joy o'erflowing.*

The text of a little song – '*Bist du bei mir*' – that he composed for her says that, should he die, he can 'go with joy, the fingers of your loving hand my eyelids gently closing'. These words give us a rare glimpse into the heart of a musician who usually preferred to express himself through his art. Incidentally, a further insight into his domestic life is provided by another, humorous, poem which says how a pipe and good tobacco pleasingly passes the time. It seems that Bach was a smoker!

Thus, at the time of Bach's second marriage all seemed to augur well for his future at Cöthen, and the receipt of a legacy of 500 guilders, expected at the time of the wedding but delayed by legal wrangles, was a welcome bonus. However, a cloud over this happiness emerged from a quite unexpected quarter. Just after his marriage, Prince Leopold also married, choosing as his bride his cousin, the Princess Friderica of Anhalt-Bernburg.

Their wedding took place at Bernburg, but when they returned to Cöthen, there were further lengthy celebrations. These perhaps passed off well, but it soon became clear to Bach that the court atmosphere was changing. The princess, as he was later to tell his old friend Georg Erdmann, proved to be 'a-musa'. (This Latin word is hard to translate, although a modern dictionary defines 'amusia' as 'the inability to comprehend or produce musical sounds'.) What he must have meant was that the princess was unmusical, uninterested in music or simply resentful of her husband's passion for an activity in which she played no part. He may therefore have seen her as unfriendly and a danger to his excellent relations with his employer. It is possible, however, that she was unhappy at Cöthen, or even unwell. Bach could not have foreseen it, but she was to die in April 1723 after just over a year of marriage.

Accordingly, and probably with sadness, Bach began again to think of leaving Cöthen for a new post, and this time his thoughts turned towards Leipzig, a city of 30,000 inhabitants where the *Kantor* of the Thomasschule, Johann Kuhnau, had died on 5 June 1722. Kuhnau's post involved the direction of the music at the city's principal churches and was one of the most important in that part of Germany. The council of the Thomaskirche met on 14 July to consider the question of his successor, and several musicians put their names forward, including Bach's old friend Telemann and some others already known to him as colleagues.

Telemann, now based in Hamburg, was offered the appointment on 13 August and accepted, but his existing employers then offered him better pay and conditions and he withdrew. On 23 November and 21 December the Thomaskirche council met again and considered five further candidates, who by this time included Bach, but then settled on Johann Christoph Graupner, a former Thomasschule pupil now working as a *Kapellmeister* at Darmstadt. But he, too, changed his mind on being offered a better deal by his current employers. While the appointment remained in the balance, the council played safe and left the door open to the other candidates, inviting Bach to perform two new cantatas for them on 7 February in the Thomaskirche. When Graupner sent his refusal in April and recommended Bach, the council offered the post to him provided that he gained his release from Cöthen. All was agreed quickly although one councillor hoped that the new man's music 'would not be theatrical'.

The story has often been told that a member of Bach's appointing committee said during these deliberations that 'since the best cannot be had we must accept the mediocre', an indication that the church worthies quite failed to recognize Bach's genius. However, the truth is that this councillor, Abraham Christoph Platz, was grouping among 'the best' (plural) Telemann, Graupner and Bach himself because all were unwilling or unable to teach Latin to the Thomasschule's choristers (as required of the *Kantor*) and it looked as if they might have to appoint an ordinary music teacher. The problem lay in the unrealistic job specification, which required a church musician who was also a pedagogue. Bach resolved the matter of teaching Latin by offering to pay a deputy to do this chore for which he was unfitted. He was later to wish that he had not been so generous.

The final stage of the negotiations took place at Cöthen and must have been painful. Bach obtained his release in the very month in which the prince's wife died. Had it not been for his marriage, Leopold would probably have kept Bach's services. As it was, he had lost both his wife and his *Kapellmeister*, and when the Bachs left (in two coaches with four wagon-loads of household goods) to move into the Thomasschule on 22 May, his once happy and lively court must have become a sadder place. Leopold himself died in November 1728 at the age of thirty-three. The Bachs and Wilhelm Friedemann attended his interment, and Bach performed a cantata in his memory. However, until Leopold's death, he and Bach remained on good terms, and Bach and his wife sometimes revisited Cöthen and performed there. Indeed, he retained the Cöthen title of *Kapellmeister von Haus aus*, literally a non-resident *Kapellmeister*.

As for the Prince, he remarried and in 1726 he and his second wife had a son to whom Bach dedicated a new harpsichord work, the six-movement *Partita in B flat*, BWV825.

CHAPTER 4

FIRST YEARS IN LEIPZIG; FRUSTRATIONS AND ACHIEVEMENTS
(1728–32)

- ♦ *Kantor at the Leipzig Thomasschule*
- ♦ *The B minor Mass*

With his move to Leipzig, says Bach's biographer Jan Chiapusso, 'Bach finally was given the opportunity to enter the career to which he had pledged himself as a young man.' But a letter which he was to write some years later, on 28 October 1730, to his friend Georg Erdmann, shows that he did not take the decision easily. It is true that in it he declared, 'God ordered it that I should be called here as Director of Music and *Kantor* at the Thomasschule', but he went on:

> *Now it seemed to me at first not at all the right thing to become a* Kantor *after being a* Kapellmeister *, and I postponed my resolution for three months; but this position was described to me as so favourable that finally (especially as my sons seemed to be inclined towards study) I risked myself in the name of the Most High and came to Leipzig, took my audition* [Probe] *and accepted the change. And here, following God's will, I have remained until now.*

As the rest of the letter shows, Bach was far from content as the *Kantor* at Leipzig's main churches and master at the Thomasschule. He still thought nostalgically of Cöthen, where he had enjoyed the patronage of 'a gracious prince who both loved and understood music, and with whom I had expected to end my days.' The purpose of his letter to Erdmann was to ask his friend, a diplomat serving in Danzig if he could help him find another job. He wrote:

> If your Honour should know of or could find a suitable situation in your city for an old and faithful servant, may I humbly request you to put in a gracious recommendation for me? For my part, I shall not fail to give satisfaction and to justify your gracious support and intercession. My present situation is worth about seven hundred thalers . . .

It is not known what reply Erdmann made to Bach's letter. Presumably he offered no prospect of an appointment in Danzig, since Bach pursued the idea no further. However, if he was willing to consider a move to a remote Baltic port, he must have been desperate to leave Leipzig. Since he had taken up his post there, much had disappointed him:

> Here, following God's will, I have remained until now. But since now, (1) I find that this post is not as remunerative as it was described to me, (2) many of the accidentia [extra fees] of the position have been withdrawn, (3) the cost of living is very high here, and (4) the authorities are strange and little interested in music, with the result that I must live with almost constant vexation, envy and harassment, I shall be compelled, with help from the Most High, to seek my fortune elsewhere.

Bach's reaction to the problems in Leipzig was by no means unpredictable. He had always had ideas of his own, and except at Cöthen, where he had been given freedom as far as his music was concerned, he had more often than not failed to get on with employers, who sometimes shook their heads even while recognizing his gifts. Things were much the same in Leipzig. The Thomasschule, where Bach lived and worked, had, like every institution, its jealousies, rivalries, quarrels and petty ambitions. Bach was never tactful in dealing with such matters. Nor was he willing to engage in intrigues, or take sides in minor disagreements. He was a distinguished church musician and proud of it, not a mere administrator. Yet the post which he now held called for him to be just that, along with being the director of music for the Thomaskirche and three other city churches. Jan Chiapusso has written:

> Bach's superiors in Leipzig would look upon his musical per-formances and compositions only as one of his duties and not with respect for the musician and the sanctity of his art, as the sensitive prince in Cöthen did. Bach was clearly aware of the strong provincialism and mediocrity of the church coun-cillors, traits which are strikingly represented by their utter failure to recognize that Bach's genius placed him far beyond the other applicants for the cantorship.

This, however, is being wise after the event. To those church councillors, Bach was no more than a senior employee, and he must have become aware of this when they interviewed him for his post. He might have been better off had he stayed at Cöthen, where, even with an unmusical princess, he would have enjoyed a civilized atmosphere and more leisure with his family, and there must have been times when he reflected bitterly that if God had summoned the princess a few months earlier, he and his wife might still be enjoying their life there. Perhaps Anna Magdalena, with her more placid temperament, told him that he had 'made his bed and must lie on it'. At least his sons could now attend the local Stadtschule, a strict institution but one with decent aca-demic standards.

His duties as *Kantor* had been described only too accurately in the contract he had signed, agreeing that he would instruct the Thomasschule boys . . .

> . . . not only in the regular classes established for that purpose, but also, without special compensation [ie extra fees], in private singing lessons. I will also faithfully attend to whatever else is incumbent upon me, and furthermore, but not without the previous knowledge and consent of a noble and most wise council, in case someone should be needed to assist me in the instruction of the Latin language, will faithfully and without ado compensate the said person out of my own pocket.

It was like signing a blank cheque, and when things started to go wrong he may have cursed himself for putting his name to it. For example, he paid fifty thalers a year to the 'third master', Carl Friedrich Pezold, to take over the Latin teaching and some other non-musical duties, and when Pezold performed badly the council's disapproval fell on Bach. He himself instructed his choristers in the Lutheran catechism as well as musical subjects, including 'theory'.

As we have seen, his overall duties as Leipzig's director of music (in full, *Cantor zu St. Thomae et Director Musices Lipsiensis*) extended not just to the Thomaskirche but also to three other churches, and a week after taking up his post in May 1723 he had performed his *Cantata No.75* at the Nikolaikirche on 30 May, Trinity Sunday. Its title was '*Die Elenden sollen essen*' ('The Wretched shall Eat'), and it was scored for voices, a trumpet, two oboes, oboe d'amore (an instrument pitched slightly lower than the normal oboe, with a mellower tone), strings and keyboard. Thus, immediately after his arrival, he was writing a new work, getting the parts copied and rehearsing and performing it with singers and instrumentalists whom he had only recently met.

His formal introduction to the staff and boys of the Thomasschule took place at 8.30 one morning. He knew that the choristers were the raw material whom he must use to carry out his duties in the Leipzig churches as well as in other areas of musical life controlled by the city authorities. Though he had failed to get on with his students as a young man in Arnstadt, he believed that he could manage these boys better, for he now had sons of his own and had become more flexible in his dealings with young people.

There were some fifty-five pupils at St Thomas's, who provided the choirs for the four churches, and Bach trained the best group to sing on alternate Sundays at the Thomaskirche and Nikolaikirche. Like choirmasters today, he selected future choristers from applicants and gave individual singing lessons, and to judge from the music he wrote for them, some of these boys must have reached a high standard. He also taught keyboard playing.

Thus, Bach's Thomasschule pupils could not only sing but also play as instrumentalists. Even so, the demands of the city churches were such that he usually had to employ members of a small group of paid city musicians amounting to four wind players, four string players and an apprentice. He also employed students from Leipzig University, for whose Paulinuskirche he sometimes provided music on festive occasions. Indeed, by the second half of 1723 he had effectively become the chief musical figure of the university and in September he applied to be formally acknowledged as Director of Music and to receive the small additional salary that went with the post. When his request was turned down by the university authorities, he appealed over their heads to the Elector of Saxony in Dresden, but although he received some sympathy, he still had to accept the compromise of being responsible only for the so-called 'old services' of feast days and academic occasions, but not for the 'new' ones of regular Sunday worship, which were left to the Nikolaikirche organist, Johann Gottlieb Görner, who was already overseeing them.

It is difficult to guess why Bach so much desired this rather poorly paid appointment, which meant extra work although also giving additional prestige. As it was, this incident made him enemies, including Görner, Bach had encroached on his territory, which he justifiably resented since Bach had a more important job and hardly needed to extend it. The university was in part to blame, for they showed a preference for Bach whenever a new celebratory cantata was needed, as in December 1726 when a new professor of law was installed and Bach composed '*Vereinigte Zwietracht der wechselnden Saiten*', BWV207. The same thing happened with another cantata, '*Entfernet euch, ihr heitern Sterne*' (now lost), written for the birthday of Elector August II of Saxony and performed before him in Leipzig's main marketplace on 12 May 1727.

The problem came to a head when the Elector's wife died in September of the same year. A university ceremony was planned and a student called Hans Carl von Kirchbach commissioned the professor of poetry, Johann Christoph Gottsched, to write the text of a tragic ode for Bach to set to music. Görner objected, claiming that he should do it, but in vain, although he was paid a small compensatory sum. This was understandable: Bach was much more talented and had already begun composing, so that even those who sympathized with Görner recognized a *fait accompli* when they saw one. Thus, on 17 October 1727, seated at the harpsichord, Bach directed the premiere of his new *Trauer Ode*, addressed in flowery language to the dead Electress Christiane Eberhardine and 'written in the Italian manner', in other words operatic in style. Görner had again been slighted, but this time he was determined to defend his position and got Bach to sign an undertaking that in future he would not enter into contracts concerning the university without proper authority.

Apart from such special occasions, the Sunday services and other church festivals, Bach also performed with his singers and instrumentalists at weddings, funerals, baptisms and civic occasions and so earned additional fees. Indeed, as his basic salary was less than a hundred thalers (much less than he had earned at Cöthen), this other work was essential. Still, he enjoyed certain benefits in kind, such as allowances for firewood, candles, corn and wine, and he and his family also lodged free in the south wing of the school. Their living quarters were cramped, but he had a big room called the *Komponirstube* or 'composition room' which was his study and office, and in which he kept the school's music library and his own.

In September 1728, Bach got into another dispute, this time with a church subdeacon who claimed his right to choose some of the music performed during Vespers (Evensong). Bach considered the choice of this music to be his business, but he lost the argument. It was hardly a serious matter, but it increased his sense of frustration. Then, in November 1730, he had to accept a reduction in the emoluments paid him for the kind of extra work mentioned above. The Thomasschule council's reason was that he was neglecting some regular duties, including the daily singing class he was contracted to give. Apparently he gave no satisfactory explanation; instead he sent them a memorandum demanding better facilities. In particular, he stated that to perform church cantatas adequately required at least a dozen competent singers plus about eighteen instrumentalists including oboes, bassoons, trumpets, timpani and a dozen string players, adding that a couple of flautists were also desirable. However, he complained, there was a general shortage of instrumentalists: he usually had only around eight and so had to seek out others from the university who had to be paid for their trouble, or use choristers whom he needed for singing. He then went on to say that only seventeen of his fifty-four Thomasschule pupils were really good enough to perform in public; as for the rest, twenty needed more training and the rest were plain incompetent. Needless to say, this was not what the council wished to hear, and his demands were ignored.

Leaving aside musical matters, the Thomasschule cannot have been much of a home for Bach and his growing family, and it is certain that he never enjoyed the part of his duties that required him to be a schoolmaster and disciplinarian. The school rules stated that:

> As soon as the bell rings (at five o'clock in summer, six in winter), each pupil must rise, wash and comb himself, and be ready in a quarter of an hour to come down for prayers bring his Bible. Clothes, shoes, stockings and linen must be kept clean. ... Before bedtime, the day's lessons must be recited and the Most High thanked for what has been learned.... Before and after midday and evening meals, the boy whose turn it is will say grace and the others will repeat it after him. During the meal shall be read aloud a Psalm or a chapter from the Bible or some other edifying book.

As for the building itself, it dated from 1553 and was draughty and uncomfortable. The boys (called *Alumnen*) were mostly from poor homes and not always in robust health or well clothed, yet besides their strict school regime and church duties they had to sing out of doors on feast days, some of which, such as Epiphany in early January, could be bitterly cold. Similarly, a Sunday service in the Thomaskirche or Nikolaikirche normally began at seven in the morning and lasted three hours. Colds (and worse illnesses) must have been endemic among the choristers and spread quickly in their cramped quarters, where they often had to share beds. Even by the standards of the time, people knew that these living conditions were inadequate, and a report of 1728 reads:

> Thirst was unbearable, especially in the hot days of summer. Further, it afflicted many poor children who, having no means of support from home, often had to climb over the water urn that stood in the chamber and drink in common with the rats, which at that time were present in frightful numbers.

The poor boys had to endure much. And not only the boys. The

Bachs' quarters were separated from theirs only by a thin wall, and although they knew of the choristers' discomfort they could do nothing to relieve it. As for the *Rektor* (headmaster), he was an aged man who had been there for four long decades and probably resisted change. Although Bach himself had been to a strict boarding school and could do without creature comforts, he must have felt that this was a poor home for his wife and family. Anna Magdalena bore him no fewer than thirteen children in this depressing place, of whom seven died in infancy.

FRUSTRATIONS AND ACHIEVEMENTS

Bach remained in his Leipzig post and was to die in the city twenty-seven years after his arrival there. Little by little, it must have become clearer to him that he would never escape to a better position, and at times he may have felt great bitterness. Yet as a deeply religious man, he seems also to have accepted that this was what God meant for him.

Despite, or perhaps because of, his unhappiness, Bach wrote music during the Leipzig years that is dazzling both in quality and sheer quantity. It has been calculated that if a professional music copyist were to set about writing the notes of all Bach's musical scores, working a thirty-five-hour week, it would take him a lifetime; Bach, of course, composed the music as well as writing and performing it. During his first ten years there, he undertook the enormous task of composing cantatas to correspond with the events of the church year, which amounted to around sixty in each year. The initial motive for this was the requirement for a cantata and a motet (a shorter vocal piece) to be performed during the long Sunday services at the Thomaskirche and Nikolaikirche, the cantata following the Gospel and preceding the Creed, and it seems to have been expected of the *Kantor* that these should be specially written rather than drawn from existing music in his library.

Accordingly, Bach composed a cantata every week, producing something like twenty minutes of music for voices and instruments, which then had to be copied (the individual parts for around sixteen singers and eighteen instrumentalists) and re-hearsed. The texts, all with biblical themes, were also specially written. Bach used several librettists, but his favourite became a man called Picander, the pen name for Christian Friedrich Henrici (1700–64), a local civil servant who composed about three hundred church cantatas at Leipzig. By 1725, Bach had written, rehearsed and performed two complete cycles of cantatas; a third followed by 1727, and a fourth by 1729 – that is, two hundred and forty substantial pieces of music in six years. By the 1740s, a fifth cycle existed. Unfortunately, around a hundred of these works have been lost, mostly the later ones, which is all the more a pity since Bach was never content simply to repeat himself and these later pieces may have had beauties that we cannot imagine.

Unbelievably, Bach also produced other church works that are towering masterpieces. There is his setting of the *Magnificat* (originally in the key of E flat) that he first performed on Christmas Day 1723 and later revised as the *Magnificat in D*, BWV243, that we know today. The *Christmas Oratorio*, BWV248, which is really a sequence of six cantatas partly adapted from earlier music, dates in its final form from the Christmas and New Year of 1734–35, when the various sections were given in turn. Similarly, the great *Mass in B minor*, BWV232, is actually made up of several pieces that he wrote independently from 1723 onwards, and finally assembled much later. He used the Kyrie and Gloria in 1733 as part of a petition to the Elector of Saxony for a court title, but the whole work as we know it today, with its five main sections (Kyrie, Gloria, Credo, Sanctus and Agnus Dei) further divided into twenty-four separate numbers, probably dates from 1749, when Bach was nearing the end of his life.

Music such as this, created under difficult conditions by a man discontented with his job, is quite extraordinary and some people react to it with the kind of wonder that expresses itself in flowery language. Thus the German scholar Fritz Volbach wrote:

> *The Bach* B minor Mass *soars above us like some huge, primitive mountain rock. Its summit is lost in the clouds in an infinity of sunlit blue, lonely and sublime, it is unapproachable by any other music. The art of Bach is one which yearns towards the eternal; through love and the grace of God it finds the way, love which entwines the transient with the everlasting, the finite with the infinite. This is a longing towards the unknown, all that is unrevealed, a longing only to be stilled by yearning. . . . Who more fitted to depict the glory of this vast heavenly kingdom, to tread this secret land of longing lying*

> *far beyond the world of reality, than J.S. Bach, the greatest German mystic?*

Fine words, but the music itself is finer. With its grandeur and gentleness, the *B minor Mass* stands as a monument of Christian sacred music, its moods ranging from the choral supplication of the opening Kyrie (in a subdued B minor) to the tremendous D major outburst of praise that is the Sanctus. No sympathetic hearer to the Credo will easily forget the drooping phrases and piercing E minor harmonies of the choral number over a throbbing bass that sets the words *Crucifixus etiam pro nobis sub Pontio Pilato, passus et sepultus est*, nor the great shout of D major joy which then follows with the words *Et resurrexit*.

'One must either believe or suspend disbelief': this was the advice given by the British tenor Sir Peter Pears in 1986 to pupils studying the solo vocal roles in Bach's *St Matthew Passion*, BWV244. This other masterpiece of the Leipzig years was first performed on Good Friday, 11 April 1727. Compared to the *B minor Mass*, it is more human and consciously dramatic, with Picander's text being not in Latin but in the German that the Leipzig congregation could understand. It tells the story of Christ's passion, beginning with the decision of the priests to arrest him and going right through to his burial. Here there are no less than seventy-eight separate musical sections, which may be long or short, solo or choral; here, too, are operatic forms such as recitative and aria as well as traditional Lutheran chorales, sometimes set with striking harmony. As for the choruses, they can represent either a faithful Christian congregation, in such solemn hymns as '*O Sacred Head sore Wounded*', or the Jerusalem crowd who yell 'Barabbas' or 'Let him be crucified!' There is no comforting resurrection message in this work intended to be heard only on Good Friday, one of the most solemn days of the Christian year. Instead it ends with a sad chorus in a minor key which is a kind of sublime sarabande, for Bach knew how to use dance styles in sacred music, just as Luther had taken folk tunes and turned them into uplifting hymns.

There is an extraordinary intensity about the music of the *St Matthew Passion*. One famous scene is that in which the disciple Peter, having been told by Jesus that he will deny him before cockcrow, does indeed do so, angrily. The Evangelist (a narrator's role given to a tenor voice) then tells us that Peter remembers Christ's words, and 'went out, and wept bitterly'. These words are sung to a long sighing phrase that is like a howl of despair. Indeed, although Bach never composed an opera, here is a work which is operatic in almost every respect. Its 'Christus' is a real role, sung by a baritone who is accompanied by the rich sound (which has been likened to a halo) of a string orchestra rather than the drier one of the harpsichord used for the Evangelist's narrative telling the story in the words of St Matthew's Gospel.

Even this great work does not stand alone, for Bach's *St John Passion*, BWV245, was composed three years earlier and first performed on Good Friday, 7 April 1724. Here, too, is powerful and profound music. Bach's biographer Malcolm Boyd says of both works that they unfold 'on four interlocking levels: the narrative (or dramatic), the lyrical, the devotional and the monumental'.

It is not surprising that between 1723 and 1729, Bach's new works were almost entirely restricted to church music. However, there are a few organ and harpsichord pieces, the former perhaps composed when he inspected new or rebuilt organs, inaugurated new ones – for example, when he went forty miles to Gera in June 1724 to play new organs in two churches, receiving a fee of thirty thalers and expenses – or simply gave recitals, as he did at the Sophienkirche in Dresden in September 1725.

Early in 1729, and apparently at his own request, Bach took over the direction of Leipzig University's *collegium musicum*, or music society. It seems that he wanted to have another area besides church music in which to work and that he found the enthusiastic, music-loving students worthy material. They performed in an outdoor coffee-garden in the summer and in Zimmermann's Coffeehouse in the winter, singing and playing all kinds of music, including Bach's. He probably performed with them some of the music that he had written at Cöthen, and composed for them two of his orchestral suites, including No.2 in B minor with its prominent flute part. (This was clearly written for a gifted young player, who perhaps also played his *Flute Sonata* in the same key, BWV1030.) The secular cantata '*Phoebus and Pan*' and the '*Coffee*' *Cantata* ('*Schweigt stille, plaudert nicht*', BWV211, also with a flute part) are genial, easy-going and above all witty pieces. The first is based on a comic tale by Ovid and the second tells of a girl whose secret but innocent passion is drinking coffee, which must have pleased Gottfried Zimmermann and his clients. Another jolly piece is the '*Peasant*' *Cantata* of 1742 ('*Mer hahn en neue Oberkeet*'), a bucolic affair using local dialect instead of formal High German and with a part for a rural-sounding horn. All three of these pieces had words by Picander, who may have found it a relief not to have to produce yet another pious church text. Bach, too, must have enjoyed this new area of his activities which allowed him to write lighter music. Although he gave up full-time direction of the *collegium musicum* in 1737, when his pupil Carl Gotthelf Gerlach took over, he kept up strong links with it.

By 1731, Bach had completed the six *Partitas*, BWV825–30, which formed the first part of the *Clavier-Übung*, and which he himself published. In 1735 he wrote his *Concerto in the Italian Style*, BWV971, a vigorous three-movement work intended for a two-manual harpsichord. Soon after this, he started to work seriously on the second book of his monumental set of forty-eight preludes and fugues, *Das Wohltemperirte Clavier*, BWV870–93, but only completed it in 1742. The title, meaning 'The Well-tempered Keyboard', refers not to good humour but to the 'equal temperament' tuning system, then fairly new, which made semitone steps on keyboard instruments equidistant and allowed any note to be a keynote. (Without this system, some keys were more 'in tune' than others.) As in the first book, here were twenty-four preludes and fugues proceeding through all the available major and minor keys. Despite the seemingly abstract nature of this enterprise, they cover a wide range of moods and show Bach's complete mastery of his craft.

In June 1730, the Thomasschule acquired a new *Rektor* following the death of the elderly incumbent. Johann Matthias Gesner at once set about an extensive rebuilding programme that improved the pupils' quarters and those of the staff. Bach must have been relieved, for his family was now numerous; in this year he proudly said that he and they could already form an ensemble of singers and players. For some months they moved out into temporary accommodation in the Hainstrasse. On reoccupying the new buildings in June 1732, Bach composed a celebratory cantata '*Froher Tag, verlangte Stunden*', 'Happy Day, Desired Hour'.

CHAPTER 5

MIDDLE YEARS IN LEIPZIG
(1730–35)

- *Petty wranglings*
- *Bach's eldest sons*

With Gesner's installation as *Rektor* in 1730, the Thomas-schule became a more congenial place for Bach and his family. The new headmaster genuinely appreciated Bach's musicianship and liked him as a man, and some years later he was to write admiringly of him at the organ, 'running over the keys of the instrument of instruments, whose innumerable pipes are brought to life by bellows, with both hands and, with the utmost speed, with his feet, producing by himself the most various and at the same time mutually agreeable combinations of sounds in orderly procession.' Gesner was no less impressed by the way his *Kantor* rehearsed his singers and players, noting that he missed nothing in the way of correctness of notes and time and liked to sing out cues to his singers. Here, he wrote, was 'this one man taking in all these harmonies with his keen ear and emitting with his voice alone the tone of all the voices. Favourer as I am of antiquity, the accomplishments of our Bach, and of any other that there may be like him, appear to me to effect what not many Orpheuses, nor twenty Arions, could achieve.'

Soon after his arrival at the Thomasschule, Gesner helped Bach by reminding his colleagues that this was not just a school but 'a seminary of music whereby the singing in all our churches might be provided'. He also obtained for him the restoration of the extra fees (*Accidentien*), which had recently been reduced by a church council puzzled by and some dissatisfied with their prickly *Kantor*. But unfortunately for Bach and his family, this gifted and ambitious man was to remain in Leipzig for only four years before he accepted a new and better post at Göttingen University.

The man who succeeded him in 1734 was much younger, and indeed, he was only three years older than Bach's oldest son Wilhelm Friedemann. He was Johann August Ernesti, a fine scholar aged twenty-seven who was already teaching at the Thomasschule. He and his *Kantor*, now nearly fifty, seem to have started on good terms and Ernesti was godfather to the Bachs' last two sons, Johann August Abraham (born in 1733) and Johann Christian (born in 1735). But before long he made clear his progressive, 'Enlightenment' views as to the Thomasschule's role in serving the church, which included the belief that music's place in worship should be that of a mere adjunct. Indeed, he treated it with some contempt, coming across a pupil practising the violin and enquiring if he, too, 'wanted to be an inn fiddler'.

Ernesti's firm priority for the Thomasschule was academic excellence, and he and his *Kantor* were soon at odds over the considerable demands that Bach placed on pupils' time for rehearsals, music-copying and the like. Then came a major clash in August 1736 over their respective spheres of authority. When Bach's choir prefect punished some younger choristers for misbehaving during a wedding service, one of them complained to Ernesti, who not only condemned the punishment but also, despite Bach's pleading, ordered the prefect to be caned in the presence of the school. Rather than accept this indignity, the prefect, who was about to go to university, left the school altogether, whereupon Ernesti, without consulting Bach, appointed a replacement choir prefect whom Bach considered to be musically inadequate and of poor character.

Bach now complained bitterly in a series of letters addressed first to the Thomasschule council, then to the Dresden church consistory, and finally to the Elector himself. His first letter, dated 12 August, begged the council to inform Ernesti that, according to the normal practice of the school, 'the *Kantor* should select choir prefects for musical competence without interference on the *Rektor*'s part'. On the same day, a Sunday, he went to his choir loft for a service, saw the unwanted new prefect (Johann

Gottlob Krause) in charge and dismissed him. But by the time of a second service later that day, Ernesti had reinstated him and on discovering this Bach drove Krause from the choir loft with 'loud cries and noise' that were heard by the waiting congregation. The next day he wrote again to the council, accusing the *Rektor* of undermining his authority, and two days later he sent them yet another letter explaining his objections to Krause. Ernesti then put his own case in writing, claiming among other things, that his *Kantor* 'should fulfil his office with greater diligence', which seems preposterous given his proven energy and capacity for work.

Bach had demanded that Ernesti be reprimanded, but the Thomasschule council did not want to offend their *Rektor*, who now made further criticisms of Bach's integrity and even veracity. Matters dragged on in what must have been a poisonous atmosphere until, on receiving a Dresden court title in November, Bach asked the consistory there to protect his position and instruct the *Rektor* accordingly. He even wrote to the Elector, asking him 'to direct the council not to molest my prerogative of appointing the *praefecto chori musici*' and 'graciously to order the consistory here to demand an apology from Rektor Ernesti for the indignity put upon me'. The Elector took Bach seriously and ordered the consistory to look into the matter with the Thomasschule council. Eventually it was decided that Ernesti should be admonished for his dealings with Bach, but that Bach, too, should be reprimanded for allowing prefects to undertake duties that he himself should have carried out, such as directing the choir at weddings. As for the wretched Krause, he was told to remain as choir prefect until he left the Thomasschule a few months later.

To the Elector of Saxony, this must have seemed a very small matter. However, he may have been genuinely sympathetic to Bach's cause, and perhaps proved it when he attended Leipzig's Easter Fair on 28 April 1738 and Bach and his *collegium musicum* performed for him. The new work was a festive secular cantata called '*Willkommen! Ihr herrschenden Götter*', and offered fulsome praise of this earthly ruler with the words 'Welcome, ye reigning gods of the earth'.

Thus Bach in his early middle-age was, as ever, a man of strong principle, pugnacious and inflexible in defending his position. Neither he nor his *Rektor* did their reputations any good by their public quarrel, but after the dust of battle had settled somehow things went on much as before, and the combatants, doubtless weary of conflict, seem to have accepted that they could continue to work together.

It was during these troubled years that Bach's oldest sons grew up. Wilhelm Friedemann was twenty in 1730 and completed his university studies three years later, going on to become the part-time organist of the Sophienkirche in Dresden. Carl Philipp Emanuel, three-and-a-half years younger, left Leipzig in 1734, when he entered the University of Frankfurt in the city of Frankfurt an der Oder. As for Johann Gottfried Bernhard, born in May 1715, when he was twenty his father managed to secure for him the post of organist at the Marienkirche in Mühlhausen, a church that had heard Bach's own music nearly three decades earlier.

Although these three sons were musically gifted, they did not automatically assume they would follow in their father's footsteps. Carl Philipp Emanuel, although he had been his father's pupil and assistant and already had several compositions to his credit by 1734, went to Frankfurt to study law rather than music. This does not necessarily mean that he planned to practise as a lawyer, or that his father forced this on him: it has rightly been said that 'his actions seem to indicate that he simply wanted to keep his options open as long as possible, and that he was guided and encouraged in that by Sebastian.' It seems certain, however, that Bach wanted his sons to have the university education that he himself had missed, knowing that it would give them the professional status without which an individual might be treated as slightingly as he had sometimes been during his own career.

In the event, Carl Philipp Emanuel did become a musician, serving in the court of King Frederick the Great of Prussia for nearly three decades from 1738–67. At the same time, he was also at home in the company of literary people and intellectuals, and acquired a lawyer-like precision in his management of money. In 1755, five years after his father's death, he applied for his Leipzig post but was unsuccessful. Eventually he succeeded Telemann as *Kantor* to the principal churches of Hamburg on the death of the older man, who, as his godfather, probably recommended.

Wilhelm Friedemann Bach's post as an organist in Dresden,

dating from 1733, came about through his father's strengthening links with that city. Bach took his *collegium musicum* of university students to Dresden from time to time, and played the fine Sophienkirche organ by Gottfried Silbermann before his son started working there. It was at this time, too, that he became friendly with the opera composer Johann Adolf Hasse (1699–1783) and, since he travelled to Dresden in September 1731 to give organ recitals in the city's churches and at court, he probably attended the premiere of Hasse's opera *Cleofide*, which took place at court on the thirteenth of that month. An early writer on Bach, Johann Nikolaus Forkel, told the story of how Bach liked to go with 'Friede' (perhaps his favourite child) to see operas and 'hear the pretty songs', and although the remark has been taken to imply condescension, it is more likely that he simply enjoyed this music. It was also in these years that he sent the Kyrie and Gloria of his *Mass in B minor* to the new Elector of Saxony, August III, with the request for a court title, mentioning the 'undeserved affronts' that he suffered in Leipzig and from which he thought a court appointment might protect him. At the time, he was unsuccessful, but on 19 November 1736 he gained the title of *Hofcompositeur* (court composer) to the Saxon court. It is understandable that he wished to see his sons rise above the pettiness of a church *Kantor*'s life under unimaginative authorities.

Unfortunately, Friedemann did not fulfil all his early promise and had a disappointing life, although he was known as a superb organist. In 1746 he was appointed to the Liebfrauenkirche in Halle, but he did not get on well there, partly because of his free-thinking turn of mind and partly because he often went in search of other posts, thus demonstrating his dissatisfaction with the one that he held. After demanding a rise in pay in 1761, receiving a curt refusal, and finally leaving his job without notice in 1764, he embarked on what was to be twenty years as a freelance teacher, organist and composer. He died in poverty, and before doing so he was reduced to selling off some of his father's manuscripts and putting J.S.Bach's name to some of his own compositions.

Although Bach did not live to see his beloved Friede's decline, he had early problems with his third son, Johann Gottfried Bernhard Bach. Soon after this young man of twenty took up his

Mühlhausen post in 1735, he fell into debt. Bach then helped him to obtain the post (perhaps better paid) of organist at the Jakobikirche in Sangerhausen, the very one that he himself had failed to obtain as a young man because of the intervention of the reigning duke in favour of another candidate; Divine Providence, he told the church council, now allowed them to give the post to a Bach, just as they had intended then. But by May 1738, Johann Bernhard was again in financial trouble and fled the town leaving unpaid bills. The mayor wrote to Bach, whom he knew, to tell him what had happened, and Bach replied in distress and embarrassment:

> *I have not set eyes on my unfortunately wayward son since last year. . . . Now I learn with the deepest dismay that he has again contracted various debts, has not in the least mended his ways, but has absconded without giving me the smallest indication of where he is staying. What more can I say or do? Since no admonition, not even loving provision and assistance, will suffice any longer, I must patiently bear my cross and simply leave my undutiful son to God's mercy, not doubting that He will hear my sorrowful prayers and finally, according to his Holy Will, bring him to know that conversion comes only from Holy Virtue. Since I have now opened my heart to Your Honour, I am fully confident that you will not impute to me the bad conduct of my son, but will recognize that a devoted father whose children are dear to him will do all he can to help promote their wellbeing. It was this that made me recommend my son, when you had the vacancy. . . . I beg Your Honour to kindly make enquiries as to his whereabouts, and then you need only give me definite information so that a final effort may be made to see if, with God's help, his obduracy can be won over and he can be made to see his errors.*

In fact, Johann Gottfried Bernhard had gone fifty miles south to Jena, where he matriculated at the University in January 1739 and intended, like Carl Philipp Emanuel, to study law. But soon after, news reached Leipzig that deeply grieved his father: he had contracted an infection and died on 27 May.

CHAPTER 6
THE LAST YEARS
(1735–50)

♦ *Increasing inner isolation*
♦ *Genius appreciated*
♦ *The Art of Fugue*

D espite the departure of three sons, Bach's household must have
been crowded at this time. When Johann Gottfried left for
Mühlhausen in 1735, four children remained whose ages ranged
between three and twenty-six, and three more were to be born
between that year and 1742. In October 1737, his nephew Johann
Elias Bach (1705–55) joined the household as a secretary and
tutor to the children; he was soon sending home to his mother
for flowers for Anna Magdalena's garden and to a friend for a tame
linnet whose singing might give her pleasure. For a gift to his
uncle, he knew that wine was always acceptable and he was happy
to offer it, and it was perhaps he who helped bring to the house
other musicians such as the lutenist Silvius Weiss, for whom Bach
may have composed his *Partita in C minor*, BWV997.

Even so, these were difficult years for the great musician,
and it has been suggested by his biographer Hannsdieter Wohlfarth that he felt an 'increasing inner isolation'. Wohlfarth suggests that 'after about 1735 he began to become aware of his
historical mission and to understand this mission as imposing
tasks he still had to fulfil'. Thus he completed and published
keyboard works (for harpsichord, or clavichord, rather than organ)
in a series that he called *Clavier-Übung*, literally 'keyboard exer-
cise'. The first volume had dated from 1731 and included the six
Partitas, while this second one had another *Partita in B minor*,
labelled 'in the French style', and the *Concerto nach italiänischen*

Gusto, nowadays usually called the *Italian Concerto* (the word *gusto* means 'taste'). The remaining two volumes of this series, published 1739–42, were to contain organ works such as the '*St Anne*' *Prelude and Fugue in E flat*, BWV552, and the *Goldberg Variations*, BWV988, a monumental set of thirty variations for harpsichord on a stately theme that Bach had written several years before.

An often-told story of this latter piece is that Bach was commissioned to write it by the Russian ambassador to Saxony, Count Keyserlingk, who suffered from insomnia and wanted music that his young harpsichordist Johann Gottlieb Goldberg (a Bach pupil) could play to him at night to help him sleep. But as Goldberg was only about fourteen and the music (written for a two-manual harpsichord) extremely difficult, it seems unlikely, although Forkel claimed that Bach received for it a golden goblet containing a hundred *louis d'or*. Another possibility is that the music is so inventive and challenging that it was intended instead to while away the count's waking hours and, at the same time, give his young harpsichordist plenty to do. Whatever the case, Bach gave the count a copy.

Although he now enjoyed some fame, Bach also met controversy, and perhaps for the first time found his achievements questioned. In May 1737 a fellow musician, Johann Adolf Scheibe, published an article that praised his compositional mastery and his artistry as a performer but declared of his works that 'his bombastic and intricate procedures deprived them of naturalness and obscured their beauty by an excess of art.' One knows what he meant: there is an ornate quality in Bach's work and sometimes an intellectual rigour that may be thought forbidding. Judged by anyone whose musical aim is simplicity and directness, Bach may be judged to fall short. Yet it has rightly been said that the problem simply 'lies in a clash of irreconcilable stylistic ideals'; other composers offer different kinds of music, but Bach had to remain himself and we should judge him in those terms. A reasoned reply to Scheibe's article was prepared by a Leipzig University lecturer called Johann Abraham Birnbaum and appeared in January 1738; Bach himself may have had a hand in it, since he distributed copies to friends.

By now, he seems to have resigned himself to staying in his Leipzig post but to have become weary of it, and someone's suggestion, in 1739, that permission might be obtained for another performance of the *St Matthew Passion* elicited from him the cool response that it had already been performed and another performance would only burden him. He might remain in his thankless position, but from now on he was, as far as possible, working for himself.

He still travelled from time to time, inspecting church organs and giving recitals. In August 1741 he went to Berlin to see his son Carl Philipp Emanuel at Frederick the Great's Potsdam court, and within a few weeks of his return he was off again, visiting Count Keyserlingk in Dresden. At home, he taught a number of gifted, carefully chosen pupils, amongst whom was Johann Christoph Altnikol (1719–59), a Leipzig University student who later married Bach's daughter Elizabeth Juliana Friederika, born in 1726. His jolly *'Peasant' Cantata* was performed on 30 August 1742 at an estate near Leipzig called Kleinzschocher, in cheerful homage to its new owner, Carl Heinrich von Dieskau. There were now very few new sacred cantatas, although Nos.197 (written for a wedding) & 200 are among them. He lost interest in such music, it seems, and was content to perform older pieces, although part of the Credo in his *B minor Mass* dates from the 1740s. In around 1745 he also began looking through some of his earlier organ pieces from the Weimar years, revising them and making a collection, BWV651–68, as well as arranging six more from movements in his church cantatas, the so-called *'Schübler' Chorales*, BWV645–50.

During the 1740s, Bach also took a keen and approving interest in the pianos being made by the organ builder Gottfried Silbermann. The pianoforte was then a new instrument and differed from the harpsichord in that its strings were struck instead of being plucked and so could play 'soft and loud', hence the name. He was to play more pianos in 1747 during the most important and best documented visit of these years, when he made his second visit to Potsdam in May of that year, probably at the invitation of King Frederick the Great himself.

He had several reasons for going. One was that his son Carl had married and he already had a grandson of eighteen months whom he wished to see; it had not been possible to go earlier because of the political differences between Prussia and Saxony. He travelled with 'Friede', who also wished to see his brother, and their encounter with the king came immediately after their arrival on Sunday, 7 May, as a contemporary newspaper account reports:

> *In the evening, at about the time when the usual chamber music began in the royal apartments, His Majesty was informed that* Kapellmeister *Bach had arrived in Potsdam and that he was at that very moment in the king's antechamber awaiting His Majesty's permission to listen to the music. The king immediately ordered that he should be allowed to enter, and as he did so His Majesty went to the so-called forte-and-piano and condescended, in person and without any preparation, to play to* Kapellmeister *Bach a theme on which to improvise a fugue. This the* Kapellmeister *did so successfully that not only was His Majesty moved to express his most gracious satisfaction with it, but all those present were astonished. Herr Bach found the theme he was given of such unusual beauty that he intends to work it out on paper as a regular fugue and have it engraved on copper. On Monday this famous man played on the organ of the Church of the Holy Ghost in Potsdam, earning universal applause from the many who heard him. In the evening His Majesty once again commanded him to execute a fugue in six parts, which he did with the same skill as on the previous occasion, to the king's satisfaction and the admiration of all.*

Some years later, Wilhelm Friedemann Bach also gave an account of these events which reminds us that Frederick the Great was a keen amateur flautist. It differs somewhat from the above account, but complements it and probably reflects events more accurately. He told Bach's biographer Forkel:

> *At this time, the king had a private concert every evening at which he generally performed some concertos on the flute. One evening, just as he was getting his flute ready and his musicians were assembled, an officer brought with him a list of the strangers who had arrived. With his flute in his hand, he ran over the list and immediately turned to the assembled musicians and said with a kind of agitation, 'Gentlemen, old Bach has come.' The flute was not laid aside and old Bach, who had alighted at his son's lodgings, was immediately summoned to the palace.*

The king gave up the evening's concert and invited Bach, then already called 'the old Bach', to try his fortepianos made by Silbermann, which stood in several rooms of the palace. The musicians went with him from room to room, and Bach was invited everywhere to try them and play unpremeditated compositions [improvisations]. After he had done so for some time, he asked the king to give him a theme for a fugue, in order to execute it immediately and without any preparation. The king admired the learned manner in which his theme was treated extempore and, probably to see how far such art could be carried, expressed a wish to hear a fugue with six obbligato parts. But as not every subject is suited to such full harmony, Bach chose one himself and immediately executed it to the astonishment of all in the same magnificent and learned manner as he had done for that of the king.

His Majesty desired also to hear his organ playing. So the next day Bach was taken to all the organs in Potsdam, as he had before been taken to Silbermann's fortepianos. After his return to Leipzig, he composed the theme which he had received from the king in three and six parts, added several composed passages in strict canon to it, had it engraved [printed] under the title 'Musical Offering' and dedicated it to its inventor.

Thus Bach, now sixty-two and nearing the end of his life, saw his genius appreciated in a way that had never seemed possible in Leipzig. His composition of the *Musikalisches Opfer*, BWV1079, which was published later in the same year and dedicated to the king, seems to acknowledge this, for in this multi-sectioned work with the royal theme at its centre he displayed his enormous command of the art to which he had dedicated his life. Some of its sections represent the noblest imaginable achievements of polyphony, although others are lighter and offer a rococo charm, with the flute (the king's instrument) often leading the proceedings.

On returning to Leipzig, Bach joined a 'Society for the Musical Sciences' founded by his former pupil Lorenz Christoph Mizler, and sent its members some intricate examples of his polyphonic art. However, according to C.P.E. Bach, he had no time for the 'dry, mathematical matters' that Mizler and his friends sometimes wanted to discuss; instead, he is supposed to have said that 'music should move the heart with sweet emotion', and never considered himself a mere intellectual.

Between 1745 and 1750, he also composed other polyphonic pieces, which are crowned by another monumental work whose very title, *The Art of Fugue*, suggests that he was making a conscious bequest to posterity and in so doing summing up his art as a composer. Having completed it, he then started work on a revision, which breaks off after some two hundred bars of a majestic fugue with four subjects, one of which is based on his own name in the German nomenclature for musical notes. (The notes are B flat, A, C and B flat natural.) C.P.E. Bach was later to write: 'Over this fugue, in which the name Bach is used as a counter-subject, its creator died.'

In his last years, Bach suffered increasingly from eye trouble: cataract affected both eyes and eventually he became completely blind. By 1749 he was no longer able to carry out his *Kantor*'s duties, and the last examples of his handwriting are very irregular. In June of that year the Thomasschule council, never tactful, invited Johann Gottlob Harrer to audition for the post of *Kantor* 'in case the *Kapellmeister* and *Kantor* Herr Sebast. Bach should die.'

In October, the now elderly and ailing musician was to have been a godfather at the birth of his Altnikol grandson, named Johann Sebastian after him, but he was unable to do so. Ever a fighter, in March 1750 he invited the English oculist John Taylor to treat his condition. However, although at first his sight improved, it quickly deteriorated again and a second unsuccessful operation left him weakened and depressed. None the less, in May he accepted into his house a new pupil, Johann Gottfried Müthel, and in July, amazingly, his sight briefly returned. On 22 July, he took what was to be his last Holy Communion, in his own home, and died six days later of a stroke.

Bach left an estate consisting of bonds and cash, manuscripts and many musical instruments, in all valued at some 1,100 thalers. But it had to be divided between his widow and his nine surviving children, and Anna Magdalena, to whom the Thomasschule council granted just six months' pension, lived for ten years in relative poverty with her unmarried stepdaughter and two younger daughters. No Thomasschule choristers sang at her funeral in 1760, but she was buried beside her husband.

Carl Philipp Emanuel Bach should perhaps have done more

to help his widowed stepmother; living in Potsdam, he may have known little of her circumstances, but seems not to have made enquiries. As for Wilhelm Friedemann, his career was already troubled and perhaps he had little spare cash to send to a stepmother. Among Anna Magdalena's own sons who later distinguished themselves as musicians, Johann Christian Bach (1735–82) inherited three of his father's harpsichords and quickly left Leipzig to go first to his brother at Potsdam and then on to Italy, where he pursued his musical studies and acquired a noble patron. He became a Catholic and an organist of Milan Cathedral, but soon found his *métier* as a composer of Italian operas. By 1762 he had received operatic offers from London, and he then made his home in the English capital, striking up a friendship there with the boy Mozart in 1764. We do not know if he ever helped his mother financially.

It was through J.C. Bach that Mozart became aware of J.S.Bach's importance. Beethoven also knew of him and once called him 'the immortal god of harmony'; the powerful fugues in his later quartets and sonatas owe much to the earlier master. But the general public had long forgotten his name when another German composer, Mendelssohn, showed, by his revival of the *St Matthew Passion* in Berlin in March 1829, that Bach's work had qualities which made it of permanent relevance to anyone who cared about music. Today this German court and church musician is universally recognized as a giant even among the great composers and is perhaps, to quote Wagner, 'the most stupendous miracle in all music'.

J.S. BACH: COMPLETE LIST OF WORKS

Bach did not number his works. They were catalogued in a thematic index by Wolfgang Schmider in 1950 and the numbers are preceded by the initials BWV, an abbreviated form of *Bach Werke-Verzeichnis*, or 'Catalogue of Bach's Works'.

Bach's church cantatas are listed here by their BWV numbers; they can, however, also be referred to by number without the BWV prefix. Some of the works ascribed to Bach in the BWV Index are now thought to be of doubtful authorship and they are not included in the following list.

Dates are given where known.

BWV1	Cantata, *Wie schön leuchtet der Morgenstern*, chorale (1725)
BWV2	Cantata, *Ach Gott, vom Himmel sieh darein*, chorale (1724)
BWV3	Cantata, *Ach Gott, wie manches, Herzeleid*, chorale (1725)
BWV4	Cantata, *Christ lag in Todes Banden*, chorale (?1707–8)
BWV5	Cantata, *Wo soll ich fliehen hin*, chorale (1724)
BWV6	Cantata, *Bleib bei uns, denn es will Abend werden* (1725)
BWV7	Cantata, *Christ unser Herr zum Jordan kam*, chorale (1724)
BWV8	Cantata, *Liebster Gott, wann werd ich sterben?*, chorale (1724)
BWV9	Cantata, *Es ist das Heil uns kommen her*, chorale (c.1732–35)
BWV10	Cantata, *Meine Seel erhebt den Herren* (1724)
BWV11	Cantata, *Lobet Gott in seinen Reichen*, Ascension Oratorio (1735)
BWV12	Cantata, *Weinen, Klagen, Sorgen, Zagen* (1714)
BWV13	Cantata, *Meine Seufzer, mein Tränen* (1726)
BWV14	Cantata, *Wär Gott nicht mit uns diese Zeit*, chorale (1735)
BWV16	Cantata, *Herr Gott, dich loben wir* (1726)
BWV17	Cantata, *Wer Dank opfert, der preiset mich* (1726)
BWV18	Cantata, *Gleichwie der Regen und Schnee vom Himmel fällt* (c.1714)
BWV19	Cantata, *Es erhub sich ein Streit* (1726)
BWV20	Cantata, *O Ewigkeit, du Donnerwort*, chorale (1724)
BWV21	Cantata, *Ich hatte viel Bekümmernis* (?1714)
BWV22	Cantata, *Jesus nahm zu sich die Zwölfe* (1723)
BWV23	Cantata, *Du wahrer Gott und Davids Sohn* (1723)
BWV24	Cantata, *Ein ungefärbt Gemüte* (1723)
BWV25	Cantata, *Es ist nicht Gesundes an meinem Leibe* (1723)

BWV26	Cantata, *Ach wie nichtig, ach wie nichtig*, chorale (1724)
BWV27	Cantata, *Wer weiss, wie nahe mir mein Ende!*, chorale (1726)
BWV28	Cantata, *Gottlob! nun geht das Jahr zu Ende* (1725)
BWV29	Cantata, *Wir danken dir, Gott, wir danken dir* (1731)
BWV30	Cantata, *Freue dich, erlöste Schar* (c.1738)
BWV30a	Cantata, *Angenehmes Widerau, freue dich* (1737)
BWV31	Cantata, *Der Himmel lacht! die Erde jubilieret* (1715)
BWV32	Cantata, *Liebster Jesu, mein Verlangen*, dialogue (1726)
BWV33	Cantata, *Allein zu dir, Herr Jesu Christ*, chorale (1724)
BWV34	Cantata, *O ewiges Feuer, O Ursprung der Liebe* (1740s)
BWV34a	Cantata, *O ewiges Feuer, O Ursprung der Liebe* (1726)
BWV35	Cantata, *Geist und Seele wird verwirret* (1726)
BWV36	Cantata, *Schwingt freudig euch empor* (1731)
BWV36a	Cantata, *Steigt freudig in die Luft* (1726)
BWV36b	Cantata, *Die Freude reget sich* (?1735)
BWV36c	Cantata, *Schwingt freudig euch empor* (1725)
BWV37	Cantata, *Wer da gläubet und getauft wird* (1724)
BWV38	Cantata, *Aus tiefer Not schrei ich zu dir*, chorale (1724)
BWV39	Cantata, *Brich dem Hungrigen dein Brot* (1726)
BWV40	Cantata, *Dazu ist erschienen der Sohn Gottes* (1723)
BWV41	Cantata, *Jesu, nun sei gepreiset*, chorale (1725)
BWV42	Cantata, *Am Abend aber desselbigen Sabbats* (1725)
BWV43	Cantata, *Gott fähret auf mit Jauchzen* (1726)
BWV44	Cantata, *Sie werden euch in die Bann tun* (1724)
BWV45	Cantata, *Es ist dir gesagt, Mensch, was gut ist* (1726)
BWV46	Cantata, *Schauet doch und sehet* (1723)
BWV47	Cantata, *Wer sich selbst erhöhet* (1726)
BWV48	Cantata, *Ich elender Mensch, wer wird mich erlösen* (1723)
BWV49	Cantata, *Ich geh und suche mit Verlangen*, dialogue (1726)
BWV50	Cantata, *Nun ist das Heil und die Kraft*
BWV51	Cantata, *Jauchzet Gott in allen Landen!* (?1730)
BWV52	Cantata, *Falsche Welt, dir trau ich nicht* (1726)
BWV54	Cantata, *Widerstehe doch der Sünde* (?1714)
BWV55	Cantata, *Ich armer Mensch, ich Sündenknecht* (1726)
BWV56	Cantata, *Ich will den Kreuzstab gerne tragen* (1726)
BWV57	Cantata, *Selig ist der Mann*, dialogue (1725)
BWV58	Cantata, *Ach Gott, wie manches Herzeleid*, dialogue, (1727)
BWV59	Cantata, *Wer mich liebet, der wird mein Wort halten* (1723–24)
BWV60	Cantata, *O Ewigkeit, du Donnerwort*, dialogue, (1723)
BWV61	Cantata, *Nun komm, der Heiden Heiland* (1714)
BWV62	Cantata, *Nun komm, der Heiden Heiland*, chorale (1724)
BWV63	Cantata, *Christen ätzet diesen Tag* (before 1716)
BWV64	Cantata, *Sehet welch eine Liebe* (1723)
BWV65	Cantata, *Sie werden aus Saba alle kommen* (1724)
BWV66	Cantata, *Erfreut euch, ihr Herzen*, dialogue (?1724)
BWV66a	Cantata, *Der Himmel dacht auf Anhalts Ruhm und Glück* (1718)
BWV67	Cantata, *Halt im Gedächtnis Jesum Christ* (1724)
BWV68	Cantata, *Also hat Gott die Welt geliebt* (1725)
BWV69	Cantata, *Lobe den Herrn, meine Seele* (1740s)
BWV69a	Cantata, *Lobe den Herrn, meine Seele* (1723)

BWV70	Cantata, *Wachet! betet! betet! wachet!* (1723)
BWV70a	Cantata, *Wachet! betet! betet! wachet!* (1716)
BWV71	Cantata, *Gott ist mein König* (1708)
BWV72	Cantata, *Alles nur nach Gottes Willen* (1726)
BWV73	Cantata, *Herr, wie du willt, so schicks mit mir* (1724)
BWV74	Cantata, *Wer mich liebet, der wird mein Wort halten* (1725)
BWV75	Cantata, *Die Elenden sollen essen* (1723)
BWV76	Cantata, *Die Himmel erzählen die Ehre Gottes* (1723)
BWV77	Cantata, *Du sollt Gott, deinen Herren, lieben* (1723)
BWV78	Cantata, *Jesu, der du meine Seele*, chorale (1724)
BWV79	Cantata, *Gott der Herr ist sonn und schild* (1725)
BWV80	Cantata, *Ein feste Burg ist unser Gott* (?1724)
BWV80a	Cantata, *Alles, was von Gott geboren* (1715)
BWV80b	Cantata, *Ein feste Burg ist unser Gott* (1723)
BWV81	Cantata, *Jesus schläft, was soll ich hoffen?* (1724)
BWV82	Cantata, *Ich habe genug* (1727)
BWV83	Cantata, *Erfreute Zeit im neuen Bunde* (1724)
BWV84	Cantata, *Ich bin vergnügt mit meinem Glücke* (1727)
BWV85	Cantata, *Ich bin ein guter Hirt* (1725)
BWV86	Cantata, *Wahrlich, wahrlich, ich sage euch* (1724)
BWV87	Cantata, *Bisher habt ihr nichts gebeten* (1725)
BWV88	Cantata, *Siehe, ich will viel Fischer aussenden* (1726)
BWV89	Cantata, *Was soll ich aus dir machen, Ephraim?* (1723)
BWV90	Cantata, *Es reisset euch ein schrecklich Ende* (1723)
BWV91	Cantata, *Gelobet seist du, Jesu Christ*, chorale (1724)
BWV92	Cantata, *Ich hab in Gottes Herz und Sinn*, chorale (1725)
BWV93	Cantata, *Wer nur den lieben Gott lässt walten*, chorale (1724)
BWV94	Cantata, *Was frag ich nach der Welt*, chorale (1724)
BWV95	Cantata, *Christus, der ist mein Leben*, chorale (1723)
BWV96	Cantata, *Herr Christ, der einige Gottessohn*, chorale (1724)
BWV97	Cantata, *In allen meinen Taten*, chorale (1734)
BWV98	Cantata, *Was Gott tut, das ist wohlgetan* (1726)
BWV99	Cantata, *Was Gott tut, das ist wohlgetan*, chorale (1724)
BWV100	Cantata, *Was Gott tut, das ist wohlgetan*, chorale (1732–35)
BWV101	Cantata, *Nimm von uns, Herr, du treuer Gott*, chorale (1724)
BWV102	Cantata, *Herr, deine Augen sehen nach dem Glauben* (1726)
BWV103	Cantata, *Ihr werdet weinen und heulen* (1725)
BWV104	Cantata, *Du Hirte Israel, höre* (1724)
BWV105	Cantata, *Herr, gehe nicht ins Gericht* (1723)
BWV106	Cantata, *Gottes Zeit ist die allerbeste Zeit*, Actus tragicus (?1707)
BWV107	Cantata, *Was willst du dich betrüben*, chorale (1724)
BWV108	Cantata, *Es ist euch gut, dass ich hingehe* (1725)
BWV109	Cantata, *Ich glaube, lieber Herr, hilf meinem Ünglauben!* (1723)
BWV110	Cantata, *Unser Mund sei voll Lachens* (1725)
BWV111	Cantata, *Was mein Gott will, das g'scheh allzeit*, chorale (1725)
BWV112	Cantata, *Der Herr ist mein getreuer Hirt*, chorale (1731)
BWV113	Cantata, *Herr Jesu Christ, du höchstes Gut*, chorale (1724)
BWV114	Cantata, *Ach, lieben Christen, seid getrost*, chorale (1724)
BWV115	Cantata, *Mache dich, mein Geist, bereit*, chorale (1724)
BWV116	Cantata, *Du Friedefürst, Herr Jesu Christ*, chorale (1724)

BWV117	Cantata, *Sei Lob und Ehr dem höchsten Gut*, chorale (c.1728–31)
BWV118	Motet, '*O Jesu Christ, mein Lebens Licht*', chorale (1736–37)
BWV119	Cantata, *Preise, Jerusalem, den Herrn* (1723)
BWV120	Cantata, *Gott, man lobet dich in der Stille* (1728–29)
BWV120a	Cantata, *Herr Gott, Beherrscher aller Dinge* (?1729)
BWV120b	Cantata, *Gott, man lobet dich in der Stille* (1730)
BWV121	Cantata, *Christum wir sollen loben schon*, chorale (1724)
BWV122	Cantata, *Das neugeborne Kindelein*, chorale (1724)
BWV123	Cantata, *Liebster Immanuel, Herzog der Frommen*, chorale (1725)
BWV124	Cantata, *Meinen Jesum lass ich nicht*, chorale (1725)
BWV125	Cantata, *Mit Fried und Freud ich fahr dahin*, chorale (1725)
BWV126	Cantata, *Erhalt uns, Herr, bei deinem Wort*, chorale (1725)
BWV127	Cantata, *Herr Jesu Christ, wahr' Mensch und Gott*, chorale (1725)
BWV128	Cantata, *Auf Christi Himmelfahrt allein* (1725)
BWV129	Cantata, *Gelobet sei der Herr, mein Gott*, chorale (1726–27)
BWV130	Cantata, *Herr Gott, dich loben alle wir*, chorale (1724)
BWV131	Cantata, *Aus der Tiefen rufe ich, Herr, zu dir* (1707)
BWV132	Cantata, *Bereitet die Wege, bereitet die Bahn!* (1715)
BWV133	Cantata, *Ich freue mich in dir*, chorale (1724)
BWV134	Cantata, *Ein Herz, das seinen Jesum lebend* (1724)
BWV134a	Cantata, *Die Zeit, die Tag und Jahre macht* (1719)
BWV135	Cantata, *Ach Herr, mich armen Sünder*, chorale (1724)
BWV136	Cantata, *Erforsche mich, Gott, und erfahre mein Herz* (1723)
BWV137	Cantata, *Lobe den Herren, den mächtigen König der Ehren*, chorale (1725)
BWV138	Cantata, *Warum betrübst du dich, mein Herz?*, chorale (1723)
BWV139	Cantata, *Wohl dem, der sich auf seinen Gott*, chorale (1724)
BWV140	Cantata, *Wachet auf, ruft uns die Stimme*, chorale (1731)
BWV144	Cantata, *Nimm, was dein ist, und gehe hin* (1724)
BWV145	Cantata, *Ich lebe, mein Herze, zu deinem, Ergötzen* (?1729)
BWV146	Cantata, *Wir müssen durch viel Trübsal* (c.1726–28)
BWV147	Cantata, *Herz und Mund und Tat und Leben* (1723)
BWV147a	Cantata, *Herz und Mund und Tat und Leben* (1716)
BWV148	Cantata, *Bringet dem Herrn Ehre seines Namens* (?1723)
BWV149	Cantata, *Man singet mit Freuden vom Sieg* (1728–29)
BWV150	Cantata, *Nach dir, Herr, verlanget mich* (c.1708–9)
BWV151	Cantata, *Süsser Trost, mein Jesus kömmt* (1725)
BWV152	Cantata, *Tritt auf die Glaubensbahn* (1714)
BWV153	Cantata, *Schau, lieber Gott, wie meine Feind* (1724)
BWV154	Cantata, *Mein liebster Jesus ist verloren* (1724)
BWV155	Cantata, *Mein Gott, wie lang, ach lange* (1716)
BWV156	Cantata, *Ich steh mit einem Fuss im Grabe* (?1729)
BWV157	Cantata, *Ich lasse dich nicht, du segnest mich denn* (1727)
BWV158	Cantata, *Der Friede sei mit dir*
BWV159	Cantata, *Sehet, wir gehn hinauf gen Jerusalem* (?1729)
BWV161	Cantata, *Komm, du süsse Todesstunde* (1715)
BWV162	Cantata, *Ach! ich sehe, jetzt, da ich zur Hochzeit gehe* (1715)
BWV163	Cantata, *Nur jedem das Seine* (1715)
BWV164	Cantata, *Ihr, die ihr eich von Christo nennet* (1725)
BWV165	Cantata, *O heilges Geist- und Wasserbad* (1715)

BWV166	Cantata, *Wo gehest du hin?* (1724)
BWV167	Cantata, *Ihr Menschen, rühmet Gottes Liebe* (1723)
BWV168	Cantata, *Tue Rechnung! Donnerwort* (1725)
BWV169	Cantata, *Gott soll allein mein Herze haben* (1726)
BWV170	Cantata, *Vergnügte Ruh', eliebte Seelenlust* (1726)
BWV171	Cantata, *Gott, wie dein Name, so ist auch dein Ruhm* (?1729)
BWV172	Cantata, *Erschallet, ihr Lieder* (1714)
BWV173	Cantata, *Erhöhtes Fliesch und Blut* (?1724)
BWV173a	Cantata, *Durchlauchtster Leopold*, serenata (?c.1722)
BWV174	Cantata, *Ich liebe den Höchsten von ganzem Gemüte* (1729)
BWV175	Cantata, *Er rufet seinen Schafen mit Namen* (1725)
BWV176	Cantata, *Es ist ein trotzig, und verzagt Ding* (1725)
BWV177	Cantata, *Ich ruf zu dir, Herr Jesu Christ*, chorale (1732)
BWV178	Cantata, *Wo Gott der Herr nicht bei uns hält*, chorale (1724)
BWV179	Cantata, *Siehe zu, dass deine Gottesfurcht* (1723)
BWV180	Cantata, *Schmücke dich, o liebe Seele*, chorale (1724)
BWV181	Cantata, *Leichtgesinnte Flattergeister* (1724)
BWV182	Cantata, *Himmelskönig, sei willkommen* (1714)
BWV183	Cantata, *Sie werden euch in den Bann tun* (1725)
BWV184	Cantata, *Erwünschtes Freudenlicht* (1724)
BWV184a	Cantata (?1722–23)
BWV185	Cantata, *Barmherziges Herze der ewigen Liebe* (1715)
BWV186	Cantata, *Ärgre dich, o Seele, nicht* (1723)
BWV186a	Cantata, *Ärgre dich, o Seele, nicht* (1716)
BWV187	Cantata, *Es wartet alles auf dich* (1726)
BWV188	Cantata, *Ich habe meine Zuversicht* (c.1728)
BWV190	Cantata, *Singet dem Herrn ein neues Lied!* (1724)
BWV190a	Cantata, *Singet dem Herrn ein neues Lied!* (1730)
BWV191	Cantata, *Gloria in exclesis Deo* (1740s)
BWV192	Cantata, *Nun danket alle Gott*, chorale (1730)
BWV193	Cantata, *Ihr Tore zu Zion* (c.1727)
BWV193a	Cantata, *Ihr Häuser des Himmels, ihr scheinenden Lichter* (1727)
BWV194	Cantata, *Höchsterwünschtes Freudenfest* (1723)
BWV194a	Cantata, (before 1723)
BWV195	Cantata, *Dem Gerechten muss das Licht* (c.1737)
BWV196	Cantata, *Der Herr denket an uns* (?1708)
BWV197	Cantata, *Gott ist unser Zuversicht* (c.1742)
BWV197a	Cantata, *Ehre sei Gott in der Höhe* (c.1728)
BWV198	Cantata, *Trauer Ode: Lass, Fürstin, lass noch einen Strahl* (1727)
BWV199	Cantata, *Mein Herze schwimmt im Blut* (1714)
BWV200	Cantata, *Bekennen will ich seinen Namen* (?c.1742)
BWV201	Cantata, *Der Streit zwischen Phoebus und Pan* (?1729)
BWV202	Cantata, *Weichet nur, betrübte Schatten* (?1718–23)
BWV204	Cantata, *Ich bin in mir vergnügt* (1726–27)
BWV205	Cantata, *Der zufriedengestellte Äolus*, dramma per musica (1725)
BWV205a	Cantata, *Blast Lärmen, ihr Feinde!* (1734)
BWV206	Cantata, *Schleicht, spielende Wellen*, dramma per musica (1736)
BWV207	Cantata, *Vereinigte Zwietracht der wechselnden Saiten*, dramma per musica (1726)
BWV207a	Cantata, *Auf, schmetternde Töne*, dramma per musica (?1735)

BWV208	Cantata, *Was mir behagt, ist nur die muntre Jagd!* (?1713)
BWV208a	Cantata, *Was mir behagt, ist nur die muntre Jagd!* (1740–42)
BWV209	Cantata, *Non sa che sia dolore* (?1734)
BWV210	Cantata, *O holder Tag, erwünschte Zeit* (c.1740)
BWV210a	Cantata, *O angenehme Melodie!* (?1738–40)
BWV211	'*Coffee*' Cantata, *Schweigt stille, plaudert nicht* (c.1734–35)
BWV212	'*Peasant*' Cantata, *Mer hahn en neue Oberkeet* (1742)
BWV213	Cantata, *Hercules auf dem Scheidewege*, dramma per musica (1733)
BWV214	Cantata, *Tönet, ihr Pauken! Erschallet, Trompeten!*, dramma per musica (1733)
BWV215	Cantata, *Preise dein Glücke, gesegnetes Sachsen*, dramma per musica (1734)
BWV216	Cantata, *Vergnügte Pleissenstadt* (1728)
BWV216a	Cantata, *Erwählte Pleissenstadt* (c.1728)
BWV223	Cantata, *Meine Seele soll Gott loben*
BWV225	Motet, '*Singet dem Herrn ein neues Lied*' (?1727)
BWV226	Motet, '*Der Geist hilft unser Schwachheit auf*' (1729)
BWV227	Motet, '*Jesu, meine Freude*' (?1723)
BWV228	Motet, '*Fürchte dich nicht*' (?1726)
BWV229	Motet, '*Komm, Jesu, komm!*' (1730)
BWV230	Motet, '*Lobet den Herrn alle Heiden*'
BWV232	*Mass*, B minor (c.1747–49)
BWV233	*Missa breve*, F major (1730s)
BWV233a	*Kyrie*, F major (1730s)
BWV234	*Missa breve*, A major (1730s)
BWV235	*Missa breve*, G minor (1730s)
BWV236	*Missa breve*, G major (1730s)
BWV237	*Sanctus*, C major (1723)
BWV238	*Sanctus*, D major (?1723)
BWV239	*Sanctus*, D minor (c.1735–46)
BWV240	*Sanctus*, G major (c.1735–46)
BWV241	*Sanctus*, D major
BWV242	*Christe eleison*
BWV243	*Magnificat*, D major (c.1728–31)
BWV243a	*Magnificat*, E flat major (1723)
BWV244	*St Matthew Passion* (c.1727–29)
BWV244a	Cantata, *Klagt, Kinder, klagt es aller Welt* (1729)
BWV245	*St John Passion* (1724)
BWV247	*St Mark Passion* (1731)
BWV248	*Christmas Oratorio* (1734–35)
BWV249	*Easter Oratorio* (1725)
BWV249a	Cantata, *Entfliehet, verschwindet, entweichet, ihr Sorgen* (1725)
BWV249b	Cantata, *Die Feier des Genius*, dramma per music (1726)
BWV250	Wedding chorale, *Was Gott tut das ist wohlgetan*
BWV251	Wedding chorale, *Sei Lob und Ehr' dem höchsten Gut*
BWV252	Wedding chorale, *Nun danket alle Gott*
BWV253	Chorale, *Ach bleibe bei uns, Herr Jesu Christ*
BWV254	Chorale, *Ach Gott, erhör' mein Seufzen*
BWV255	Chorale, *Ach Gott und Herr*
BWV256	Chorale, *Ach lieben Christen, seid getrost*

BWV257	Chorale, *Wär' Gott nicht mit uns diese Zeit*
BWV258	Chorale, *Wo Gott der Herr nicht bei uns hält*
BWV259	Chorale, *Ach, was soll ich Sünder machen*
BWV260	Chorale, *Allein Gott in der Höh' sei Ehr'*
BWV261	Chorale, *Allein zu dir, Herr Jesu Christ*
BWV262	Chorale, *Alle Menschen müssen sterben*
BWV263	Chorale, *Alles ist an Gottes Segen*
BWV264	Chorale, *Als der gütige Gott*
BWV265	Chorale, *Als Jesus Christus in der Nacht*
BWV266	Chorale, *Als vierzig Tag nach Ostern*
BWV267	Chorale, *An Wasserflüssen Babylon*
BWV268	Chorale, *Auf, auf, mein Herz, und du mein ganzer Sinn*
BWV269	Chorale, *Aus meines Herzens Grunde*
BWV270	Chorale, *Befiehl du deine Wege*
BWV271	Chorale, *Befiehl du deine Wege*
BWV272	Chorale, *Befiehl du deine Wege*
BWV273	Chorale, *Christ, der du bist der helle Tag*
BWV274	Chorale, *Christe, der due bist Tag und Licht*
BWV275	Chorale, *Christe, du Beistand deiner Kreuzgemeinde*
BWV276	Chorale, *Christe ist erstanden*
BWV277	Chorale, *Christ lag in Todesbanden*
BWV278	Chorale, *Christ lag in Todesbanden*
BWV279	Chorale, *Christ lag in Todesbanden*
BWV280	Chorale, *Christ, unser Herr, zum Jordan kam*
BWV281	Chorale, *Christus, der ist mein Leben*
BWV282	Chorale, *Christus, der ist mein Leben*
BWV283	Chorale, *Christus, der uns selig macht*
BWV284	Chorale, *Christus ist erstanden, hat überwunden*
BWV285	Chorale, *Da der Herr Christ zu Tische sass*
BWV286	Chorale, *Danket dem Herrne*
BWV287	Chorale, *Dank sei Gott in der Höhe*
BWV288	Chorale, *Das alte Jahr vergangen ist*
BWV289	Chorale, *Das alte Jahr vergangen ist*
BWV290	Chorale, *Das walt' Gott Vater und Gott Sohn*
BWV291	Chorale, *Das walt' mein Gott, Vater, Sohn und heiliger Geist*
BWV292	Chorale, *Den Vater dort oben*
BWV293	Chorale, *Der du bist drei in Einigkeit*
BWV294	Chorale, *Der Tag, der ist so freudenreich*
BWV295	Chorale, *Des heil'gen Geistes reiche Gnad'*
BWV296	Chorale, *Die Nacht ist kommen*
BWV297	Chorale, *Die Sonn' hat sich mit ihrem Glanz*
BWV298	Chorale, *Dies sind die heil'gen zehn Gebot'*
BWV299	Chorale, *Dir, dir, Jehova, will ich singen*
BWV300	Chorale, *Due grosser Schmerzensmann*
BWV301	Chorale, *Du, o schönes Welgebäude*
BWV302	Chorale, *Ein' feste Burg ist unser Gott*
BWV303	Chorale, *Ein' feste Burg ist unser Gott*
BWV304	Chorale, *Eins ist Not! ach Herr, dies Eine*
BWV305	Chorale, *Erbarm' dich mein, o Herre Gott*
BWV306	Chorale, *Erstanden ist der Heil'ge Christ*

BWV307	Chorale, *Es ist gewisslich an der Zeit*
BWV308	Chorale, *Es spricht der Unweisen Mund wohl*
BWV309	Chorale, *Es stehn vor Gottes Throne*
BWV310	Chorale, *Es wird schier der letzte Tag herkommen*
BWV311	Chorale, *Es woll' uns Gott genädig sein*
BWV312	Chorale, *Es woll' uns Gott genädig sein*
BWV313	Chorale, *Für Freuden lasst uns springen*
BWV314	Chorale, *Gelobet seist du, Jesu Christ*
BWV315	Chorale, *Gib dich zufrieden und sei stille*
BWV316	Chorale, *Gott der du selber bist das Licht*
BWV317	Chorale, *Gott, der Vater, wohn' uns bei*
BWV318	Chorale, *Gottes Sohn ist kommen*
BWV319	Chorale, *Gott hat das Evangelium*
BWV320	Chorale, *Gott lebet noch*
BWV321	Chorale, *Gottlob, es geht nunmehr zu Ende*
BWV322	Chorale, *Gott sei gelobet und gebendedeiet*
BWV323	Chorale, *Gott sei uns gnädig*
BWV325	Chorale, *Heilig, heilig*
BWV326	Chorale, *Herr Gott, dich loben alle wir*
BWV327	Chorale, *Für deinen Thron tret' ich hiermit*
BWV328	Chorale, *Herr Gott, dich loben wir*
BWV329	Chorale, *Herr, ich denk' an jene Zeit*
BWV330	Chorale, *Herr, ich habe missgehandelt*
BWV331	Chorale, *Herr, ich habe missgehandelt*
BWV332	Chorale, *Herr Jesu Christ, dich zu uns wend'*
BWV333	Chorale, *Herr Jesu Christ, du hast bereit't*
BWV334	Chorale, *Herr Jesu Christ, du höchstes Gut*
BWV335	Chorale, *Herr Jesu Christ, mein's Lebens Licht*
BWV336	Chorale, *Herr Jesu Christ, wahr'r Mensch und Gott*
BWV337	Chorale, *Herr, nun lass in Frieden*
BWV338	Chorale, *Herr, straf mich nicht in deinem Zorn*
BWV339	Chorale, *Herr, wie du willst, so schick's mit mir*
BWV340	Chorale, *Herzlich lieb hab ich dich, o Herr*
BWV341	Chorale, *Heut' ist, o Mensch, ein grosser Trauertag*
BWV342	Chorale, *Heut' triumphieret Gottes Sohn*
BWV343	Chorale, *Hilf, Gott, dass mir's gelinge*
BWV344	Chorale, *Hilf, Herr Jesu, lass gelingen*
BWV345	Chorale, *Ich bin ja, Herr, in deiner Macht*
BWV346	Chorale, *Ich dank' dir, Gott, für all' Wohltat*
BWV347	Chorale, *Ich dank' dir, lieber Herre*
BWV348	Chorale, *Ich dank' dir, lieber Herre*
BWV349	Chorale, *Ich dank' dir schon durch deinen Sohn*
BWV350	Chorale, *Ich danke dir, o Gott, in einem Throne*
BWV351	Chorale, *Ich hab' mein' Sach' Gott heimgestellt*
BWV352	Chorale, *Jesu, der du meine Seele*
BWV353	Chorale, *Jesu, der du meine Seele*
BWV354	Chorale, *Jesu, der du meine Seele*
BWV355	Chorale, *Jesu, der du selbsten wohl*
BWV356	Chorale, *Jesu, du mein liebstes Leben*
BWV357	Chorale, *Jesu, Jesu, du bist mein*

BWV358	Chorale, *Jesu, meine Freude*
BWV359	Chorale, *Jesu meiner Seelen Wonne*
BWV360	Chorale, *Jesu meiner Seelen Wonne*
BWV361	Chorale, *Jesu, meines Herzens Freud'*
BWV362	Chorale, *Jesu, nun sei gepreiset*
BWV363	Chorale, *Jesu Christus, unser Heiland*
BWV364	Chorale, *Jesu Christus, unser Heiland*
BWV365	Chorale, *Jesus, meine Zuversicht*
BWV366	Chorale, *Ihr Gestirn', ihr hohlen Lüfte*
BWV367	Chorale, *In allen meinen Taten*
BWV368	Chorale, *In dulci jubilo*
BWV369	Chorale, *Keinen hat Gott verlassen*
BWV370	Chorale, *Komm, Gott Schöpfer, heiliger Geist*
BWV371	Chorale, *Kyrie, Gott Vater in Ewigkeit*
BWV372	Chorale, *Lass, o Herr, dein Ohr sich neigen*
BWV373	Chorale, *Liebster Jesu, wir sind hier*
BWV374	Chorale, *Lobet den Herren, denn er ist freundlich*
BWV375	Chorale, *Lobt Gott, ihr Christen, allzugleich*
BWV376	Chorale, *Lobt Gott, ihr Christen, allzugleich*
BWV377	Chorale, *Mach's mit mir, Gott, nach deiner Güt'*
BWV378	Chorale, *Meine Augen schliess' ich jetzt*
BWV379	Chorale, *Meinen Jesum lass' ich nicht, Jesus*
BWV380	Chorale, *Meinen Jesum lass' ich nicht, weil*
BWV381	Chorale, *Meines Lebens letzte Zeit*
BWV382	Chorale, *Mit Fried' und Freud' ich fahr' dahin*
BWV383	Chorale, *Mitten wir im Leben sind*
BWV384	Chorale, *Nicht so traurig, nicht so sehr*
BWV385	Chorale, *Nun bitten wir den heiligen Geist*
BWV386	Chorale, *Nun danket alle Gott*
BWV387	Chorale, *Nun freut euch, Gottes Kinder all'*
BWV388	Chorale, *Nun freut euch, lieben Christen, g'mein*
BWV389	Chorale, *Nun lob', mein' Seel', den Herren*
BWV390	Chorale, *Nun lob', mein' Seel', den Herren*
BWV391	Chorale, *Nun preiset alle Gottes Barmherzigkeit*
BWV392	Chorale, *Nun ruhen alle Wälder*
BWV393	Chorale, *O Welt, sieh hier dein Leben*
BWV394	Chorale, *O Welt, sieh hier dein Leben*
BWV395	Chorale, *O Welt, sieh hier dein Leben*
BWV396	Chorale, *Nun sich der Tag geendet hat*
BWV397	Chorale, *O Ewigkeit, du Donnerwort*
BWV398	Chorale, *O Gott du frommer Gott*
BWV399	Chorale, *O Gott du frommer Gott*
BWV400	Chorale, *O Herzensangst, o Bangigkeit*
BWV401	Chorale, *O Lamm Gottes, unschuldig*
BWV402	Chorale, *O Mensch, bewein' dein' Sünde gross*
BWV403	Chorale, *O Mensch, schau Jesum Christum an*
BWV404	Chorale, *O Traurigkeit, o Herzeleid*
BWV405	Chorale, *O wie selig seid ihr doch, ihr Frommen*
BWV406	Chorale, *O wie selig seid ihr doch, ihr Frommen*
BWV407	Chorale, *O wir armen Sünder*

BWV408	Chorale, *Schaut, ihr Sünder*
BWV409	Chorale, *Seelen-Bräutigam*
BWV410	Chorale, *Sei gegrüsset, Jesu gütig*
BWV411	Chorale, *Singet dem Herrn ein neues Lied*
BWV412	Chorale, *So gibst du nun, mein Jesu, gute Nacht*
BWV413	Chorale, *Sollt' ich meinem Gott nicht singen*
BWV414	Chorale, *Uns ist ein Kindlein heut' gebor'n*
BWV415	Chorale, *Valet will ich dir geben*
BWV416	Chorale, *Vater unser im Himmelreich*
BWV417	Chorale, *Von Gott will ich nicht lassen*
BWV418	Chorale, *Von Gott will ich nicht lassen*
BWV419	Chorale, *Von Gott will ich nicht lassen*
BWV420	Chorale, *Warum betrübst du dich, mein Herze*
BWV421	Chorale, *Warum betrübst du dich, mein Herze*
BWV422	Chorale, *Warum sollt' ich mich denn grämen*
BWV423	Chorale, *Was betrübst du dich, mein Herze*
BWV424	Chorale, *Was bist du doch, o Seele, so betrübet*
BWV425	Chorale, *Was willst du dich, o mein Seele*
BWV426	Chorale, *Weltlich Ehr' und zeitlich Gut*
BWV427	Chorale, *Wenn ich in Angst und Not*
BWV428	Chorale, *Wenn mein Stündlein vorhanden ist*
BWV429	Chorale, *Wenn mein Stündlein vorhanden ist*
BWV430	Chorale, *Wenn mein Stündlein vorhanden ist*
BWV431	Chorale, *Wenn wir in höchsten Nöten sein*
BWV432	Chorale, *Wenn wir in höchsten Nöten sein*
BWV433	Chorale, *Wer Gott vertraut, hat wohl gebaut*
BWV434	Chorale, *Wer nur den lieben Gott lässt walten*
BWV435	Chorale, *Wie bist du, Seele, in mir so gar betrübt*
BWV436	Chorale, *Wie schön leuchtet der Morgenstern*
BWV437	Chorale, *Wir glauben all' an einen Gott*
BWV438	Chorale, *Wo Gott zum Haus nicht gibt sein' Gunst*
BWV439	Chorale, *Ach, dass nicht die letzte Stunde*
BWV440	Chorale, *Auf, auf! die rechte Zeit ist hier*
BWV441	Chorale, *Auf, auf! mein Herz, mit Freuden*
BWV442	Chorale, *Beglücketer Stand getreuer Seelen*
BWV443	Chorale, *Beschränkt, ihr Weisen dieser Welt*
BWV444	Chorale, *Brich entzwei, mein armes Herze*
BWV445	Chorale, *Brunnquell aller Güter*
BWV446	Chorale, *Der lieben Sonnen Licht und Pracht*
BWV447	Chorale, *Der Tag ist hin, die Sonne gehet nieder*
BWV448	Chorale, *Der Tag mit seinem Lichte*
BWV449	Chorale, *Dich bet'ich an, mein höchster Gott*
BWV450	Chorale, *Die bittre Leidenszeit beginnet abermal*
BWV451	Chorale, *Die goldne Sonne, voll Freud' und Wonne*
BWV452	Chorale, *Dir, dir Jehovan, will ich singen*
BWV453	Chorale, *Eins ist Not! ach Herr, dies Eine*
BWV454	Chorale, *Ermuntre dich, mein schwacher Geist*
BWV455	Chorale, *Erwürgtes Lamm, das die verwahrten Siegel*
BWV456	Chorale, *Es glänzet der Christen*
BWV457	Chorale, *Es ist nun aus mit meinem Leben*

BWV458 Chorale, *Es ist vollbracht! vergiss ja nicht*
BWV459 Chorale, *Es kostet viel, ein Christ zu sein*
BWV460 Chorale, *Gieb dich zufrieden und sei stille*
BWV461 Chorale, *Gott lebet noch: Seele, was verzagst du doch?*
BWV462 Chorale, *Gott, wie gross ist deine Güte*
BWV463 Chorale, *Herr, nicht schicke deine Rache*
BWV464 Chorale, *Ich bin ja, Herr, in deiner Macht*
BWV465 Chorale, *Ich freue mich in der*
BWV466 Chorale, *Ich halte treulich still und liebe*
BWV467 Chorale, *Ich lass' dich nicht*
BWV468 Chorale, *Ich liebe Jesum alle Stund'*
BWV469 Chorale, *Ich steh' an deiner Krippen hier*
BWV470 Chorale, *Jesu, Jesu, du bist mein*
BWV471 Chorale, *Jesu, deine Liebeswunden*
BWV472 Chorale, *Jesu, meines Glaubens Zier*
BWV473 Chorale, *Jesu, meines Herzens Freud'*
BWV474 Chorale, *Jesus ist das schönste Licht*
BWV475 Chorale, *Jesus, unser Trost und Leben*
BWV476 Chorale, *Ihr Gestirn', ihr hohen Lüfte*
BWV477 Chorale, *Kein Stündlein geht dahin*
BWV478 Chorale, *Komm, süsser Tod, komm, sel'ge Ruh'!*
BWV479 Chorale, *Kommt, Seelen, dieser Tag*
BWV480 Chorale, *Kommt wieder aus der finstern Gruft*
BWV481 Chorale, *Lasset, uns mit Jesu ziehen*
BWV482 Chorale, *Liebes Herz, bedenke doch*
BWV483 Chorale, *Liebster Gott, wann werd' ich sterben?*
BWV484 Chorale, *Liebster Herr Jesu! wo bleibest du so lange?*
BWV485 Chorale, *Liebster Immanuel, Herzog der Frommen*
BWV486 Chorale, *Mein Jesu, dem die Seraphinen*
BWV487 Chorale, *Mein Jesu? was für Seelenweh*
BWV488 Chorale, *Meines Lebens letzte Zeit*
BWV489 Chorale, *Nicht so traurig nicht so sehr*
BWV490 Chorale, *Nur mein Jesus ist mein Leben*
BWV491 Chorale, *O du Liebe meine Liebe*
BWV492 Chorale, *O finstre Nacht*
BWV493 Chorale, *O Jesulein süss, o Jesulein mild*
BWV494 Chorale, *O liebe Seele, zieh' die Sinnen*
BWV495 Chorale, *O wie selig seid ihr doch, ihr Frommen*
BWV496 Chorale, *Seelen-Bräutigam, Jesu, Gottes Lamm!*
BWV497 Chorale, *Seelenweide, meine Freude*
BWV498 Chorale, *Selig, wer an Jesum denkt*
BWV499 Chorale, *Sei gegrüsset, Jesu gütig*
BWV500 Chorale, *So gehst du nun, mein Jesu, hin*
BWV501 Chorale, *So giebst du nun, mein Jesu, gute Nacht*
BWV502 Chorale, *So wünsch' ich mir zu guter Letz*
BWV503 Chorale, *Steh' ich bei meinem Gott*
BWV504 Chorale, *Vergiss mein nicht, dass ich dein nicht*
BWV505 Chorale, *Vergiss mein nicht, vergiss mein nicht*
BWV506 Chorale, *Was bist du doch, o Seele, so betrübet*
BWV507 Chorale, *Wo ist mein Schäflein, das ich liebe*

BWV511	Chorale, *Gib dich zufrieden*, Clavier-büchlein, ii, for Anna Magdalena Bach (1722–25)
BWV512	Chorale, *Gib dich zufrieden*, Clavier-büchlein, ii, for Anna Magdalena Bach (1722–25)
BWV513	Chorale, *O Ewigkeit, du Donnerwort*, Clavier-büchlein, ii, for Anna Magdalena Bach (1722–25)
BWV515b	Aria, '*So oft ich mein Tobackspfeife*', Clavierbüchlein, ii, for Anna Magdalena Bach (1722–25)
BWV518	Aria, '*Willst du dein Merz mir schenken*', '*Aria di Giovanni*', Clavierbüchlein, ii, for Anna Magdalena Bach (1722–25)
BWV524	Fragment (1707)
BWV525	*Trio Sonata*, organ, E flat major (c.1727)
BWV526	*Trio Sonata*, organ, C minor (c.1727)
BWV527	*Trio Sonata*, organ, D minor (c.1727)
BWV528	*Trio Sonata*, organ, E minor (c.1727)
BWV529	*Trio Sonata*, organ, C major (c.1727)
BWV530	*Trio Sonata*, organ, G major (c.1727)
BWV531	*Prelude and fugue*, organ, C major (?1707)
BWV532	*Prelude and fugue*, organ, D major (1708–17)
BWV533	*Prelude and fugue*, organ, E minor (?1708)
BWV534	*Prelude and fugue*, organ, F minor (1708–17)
BWV535	*Prelude and fugue*, organ, G minor (1708–17)
BWV536	*Prelude and fugue*, organ, A major (1708–17)
BWV537	*Fantasia and fugue*, organ, C minor (1708–17)
BWV538	*Toccata and fugue*, organ, 'Dorian', D minor (1708–17)
BWV539	*Prelude and fugue*, organ, D minor (1720s)
BWV540	*Toccata and fugue*, organ, F major (1708–17)
BWV541	*Prelude and fugue*, organ, G major (1708–17)
BWV542	*Fantasia and fugue*, organ, G minor (1708–25)
BWV543	*Prelude and fugue*, organ, A minor (1708–17)
BWV544	*Prelude and fugue*, organ, B minor (1727–31)
BWV545	*Prelude and fugue*, organ, C major (1708–17)
BWV546	*Prelude and fugue*, organ, C minor (1708–17)
BWV547	*Prelude and fugue*, organ, C major (after 1723)
BWV548	*Prelude and fugue*, organ, E minor (1727–31)
BWV549	*Prelude and fugue*, organ, C minor (1708–17)
BWV550	*Prelude and fugue*, organ, G major (before 1708)
BWV551	*Prelude and fugue*, organ, A minor (before 1708)
BWV552	*Prelude and fugue*, organ, '*St Anne*', E flat major, Clavier-Übung, iii (1739)
BWV562	*Fantasia and fugue*, organ, C minor (1708–17; c.1745)
BWV563	*Fantasia*, organ, B minor (before 1707)
BWV564	*Toccata*, adagio and fugue, organ, C major (1708–17)
BWV565	*Toccata and fugue*, organ, D minor (before 1708)
BWV566	*Prelude and fugue*, organ, E major (before 1708)
BWV568	*Prelude*, organ, G major (before 1708)
BWV569	*Prelude*, organ, A minor (before 1708)
BWV570	*Fantasia*, organ, C major (before 1707)
BWV572	*Fantasia*, organ, G major (before 1708)

BWV573	*Fantasia*, organ, C major, Clavier-Büchlein, i, for Anna Magdalena Bach (c.1722)
BWV574	*Fugue on theme by Legrenzi*, C minor
BWV575	*Fugue*, organ, C minor (?1708–17)
BWV578	*Fugue*, organ, G minor (?1707)
BWV579	*Fugue on theme by Corelli*, B minor
BWV582	*Passacaglia*, organ, C minor
BWV583	*Trio*, organ, D minor
BWV586	*Trio*, organ, G major
BWV587	*Aria*, organ, F major
BWV588	*Canzona*, organ, D minor (c.1715)
BWV590	*Pastorale*, organ, F major (c.1710)
BWV592	*Organ Concerto*, G major (1708–17)
BWV593	*Organ Concerto*, A minor (1708–17)
BWV594	*Organ Concerto*, C major (1708–17)
BWV595	*Organ Concerto*, C major (1708–17)
BWV596	*Organ Concerto*, D minor (1708–17)
BWV597	*Organ Concerto*, E flat major (1708–17)
BWV598	*Pedal-Exercitium* for organ

Das Orgel-Büchlein (c.1713–17)

BWV599	*Nun komm' der Heiden Heiland*
BWV600	*Gott, durch deine Güte*
BWV601	*Herr Christ, der ein'ge Gottes-Sohn*
BWV602	*Lob sei dem allmächtigen Gott*
BWV603	*Puer natus in Bethlehem*
BWV605	*Der Tag, der ist so freudenreich*
BWV606	*Vom Himmel hoch da komm' ich her*
BWV607	*Vom Himmel kam der Engel Schar*
BWV608	*In dulci jubilo*
BWV609	*Lobt Gott, ihr Christen, allzugleich*
BWV610	*Jesu, meine Freude*
BWV611	*Christum wir sollen loben schon*
BWV612	*Wir Christenleut'*
BWV613	*Helft mir Gottes Güte preisen*

—

BWV614	*Das alte Jahr vergangen ist*, Das Orgel-Büchlein (1740s)

Das Orgel-Büchlein (c.1713–17)

BWV615	*In dir ist Freude*
BWV616	*Mit Fried' und Freud' ich fahr dahin*
BWV617	*Herr Gott, nun schleuss den Himmel auf*
BWV618	*O Lamm Gottes unschuldig*
BWV619	*Christe, du Lamm Gottes*
BWV620	*Christus, der uns selig macht*
BWV621	*Da Jesus an dem Kreuze stund'*
BWV622	*O Mensch, bewein' dein' Sünde gross*
BWV623	*Wir danken dir, Herr Jesu Christ*
BWV624	*Elf Gott, dass mir's gelinge*
BWV625	*Christ lag in Todesbanden*

BWV626	*Jesus Christus, unser Heiland*
BWV627	*Christ ist erstanden*
BWV628	*Erstanden ist der heil'ge Christ*
BWV629	*Erschienen ist der herrliche Tag*
BWV630	*Heut' triumphieret Gottes Sohn*
BWV631	*Komm, Gott Schöpfer, heiliger Geist*
BWV632	*Herr Jesu Christ, dich zu uns wend'*
BWV633	*Liebster Jesu, wir sind hier*
BWV635	*Dies sind die heil'gen zehn Gebot'*
BWV636	*Vater unser im Himmelreich*
BWV637	*Durch Adam's Fall ist ganz verderbt*
BWV638	*Es ist das Heil uns kommen her*
BWV639	*Ich ruf' zu dir, Herr Jesu Christ*
BWV640	*In dich hab' ich gehoffet, Herr*
BWV641	*Wenn wir in höchsten Nöten sein*
BWV642	*Wer nur den lieben Gott lässt walten*
BWV643	*Alle Menschen müssen sterben*
BWV644	*Ach wie nichtig, ach wie flüchtig*

—

BWV645	*Wachet auf, ruft uns die Stimme*, Sechs Choräle ['*Schübler*' *chorale*] (c.1748–49)
BWV646	*Wo soll ich fliehen hin*, Sechs Choräle ['*Schübler*' *chorale*] (c.1748–49)
BWV647	*Wer nur den lieben Gott lässt walten*, Sechs Choräle ['*Schübler*' *chorale*] (c.1748–49)
BWV648	*Meine Seele erhebet den Herren*, Sechs Choräle ['*Schübler*' *chorale*] (c.1748–49)
BWV649	*Ach bleib' bei uns, Herr Jesu Christ*, Sechs Choräle ['*Schübler*' *chorale*] (c.1748–49)
BWV650	*Kommst du nun Jesu, vom Himmel herunter*, Sechs Choräle ['*Schübler*' *chorale*] (c.1748–49)
BWV651	Chorale, *Fantasia super Komm, Heiliger Geist* (1708–17)
BWV652	Chorale, *Komm, Heiliger Geist* (1708–17)
BWV653	Chorale, *An Wasserflüssen Babylon* (1708–17)
BWV654	Chorale, *Schmücke, dich, o liebe Seele* (1708–17)
BWV655	Chorale, *Trio super Herr Jesu Christ, dich zu uns wend* (1708–17)
BWV656	Chorale, *O Lamm Gottes unschuldig* (1708–17)
BWV657	Chorale, *Nun danket alle Gott* (1708–17)
BWV658	Chorale, *Von Gott will ich nicht lassen* (1708–17)
BWV659	Chorale, *Nun komm, der Heiden Heiland* (1708–17)
BWV660	Chorale, *Trio super Nun komm, der Heiden Heiland* (1708–17)
BWV661	Chorale, *Nun komm, der Heiden Heiland* (1708–17)
BWV662	Chorale, *Allein Gott in der Höh sei Ehr* (1708–17)
BWV663	Chorale, *Allein Gott in der Höh sei Ehr* (1708–17)
BWV664	Chorale, *Trio super Allein Gott in der Höh sei Ehr* (1708–17)
BWV665	Chorale, *Jesus Christus, unser Heiland* (1708–17)
BWV666	Chorale, *Jesus Christus, unser Heiland* (1708–17)

BWV667   Chorale, *Komm, Gott, Schöpfer, Heiliger Geist* (1708–17)
BWV668   Chorale, *Wenn wir in hoechsten Noeten sein* (c.1744–47)

Chorale preludes in Clavier-Übung, iii (1739)

BWV669   *Kyrie, Gott Vater in Ewigkeit,*
BWV670   *Christe, aller Welt Trost*
BWV671   *Kyrie, Gott heiliger Geist*
BWV672   *Kyrie, Gott Vater in Ewigkeit*
BWV673   *Christe, aller Welt Trost*
BWV674   *Kyrie, Gott heiliger Geist*
BWV675   *Allein Gott in der Höh sei Ehr*
BWV676   *Allein Gott in der Höh sei Ehr*
BWV677   *Fughetta super Allein Gott in der Höh sei Ehr*
BWV678   *Dies sind die heilgen zehen Gebot*
BWV679   *Fughetta super Dies sind die heiligen zeben Gebot*
BWV680   *Wir gläuben all an einen Gott*
BWV681   *Fughetta super Wir gläuben all an einen Gott*
BWV682   *Vater unser im Himmelreich*
BWV683   *Vater unser im Himmelreich*
BWV684   *Christ, unser Herr, zum Jordan kam*
BWV685   *Christ, unser Herr, zum Jordan kam*
BWV686   *Aus tiefer Not schrei ich zu dir*
BWV687   *Aus tiefer Not schrei ich zu dir*
BWV688   *Jesus Christus, unser Heiland, der von uns den Zorn Gottes wandt*
BWV689   *Fuga super Jesus Christus unser Heiland*

—

BWV690   *Wer nur den lieben Gott lässt walten* (1708–17)
BWV691   *Wer nur den lieben Gott lässt walten*, Clavier-Büchlein for W.F. Bach (1720–)
BWV694   *Wo soll ich flieben hin* (before 1708)
BWV695   *Fantasia super Christ lag in Todes Banden* (?1708–17)
BWV696   *Christum wir sollen loben schon* (?1708–17)
BWV697   *Gelobet seist du, Jesu Christ* (?1708–17)
BWV698   *Herr Christ, der einig Gottes Sohn* (?1708–17)
BWV699   *Nun komm, der Heiden Heiland* (?1708–17)
BWV700   *Vom Himmel hoch, da komm ich her* (?1708)
BWV701   *Vom Himmel hoch, da komm ich her* (?1708–17)
BWV703   *Gottes Sohn ist kommen* (?1708–17)
BWV704   *Lob sei dem allmächtigen Gott* (?1708–17)
BWV706   *Liebster Jesu, wir sind hier* (1708–17)
BWV709   *Herr Jesu Christ, dich zu uns wend* (?1708–17)
BWV710   *Wir Christenleut habn jetzund Freud* (?1708–17)
BWV711   *Allein Gott in der Höh sei Ehr* (?1708–17)
BWV712   *In dich hab ich gehoffet, Herr* (?1708–17)
BWV713   *Fantasia super Jesu, meine Freud* (?1708–17)
BWV714   *Ach Gott und Herr* (?1708–17)
BWV715   *Allein Gott in der Höh sei Ehr* (1703–8 or 1708–17)
BWV717   *Allein Gott in der Höh sei Ehr* (1708–17)
BWV718   *Christ lag in Todes Banden* (before 1708)
BWV720   *Ein feste Burg ist unser Gott* (1709)

BWV791	*Sinfonia*, E flat major
BWV792	*Sinfonia*, E major
BWV793	*Sinfonia*, E minor
BWV794	*Sinfonia*, F major
BWV795	*Sinfonia*, F minor
BWV796	*Sinfonia*, G major
BWV797	*Sinfonia*, G minor
BWV798	*Sinfonia*, A major
BWV799	*Sinfonia*, A minor
BWV800	*Sinfonia*, B flat major
BWV801	*Sinfonia*, B minor

—

BWV802	*Duetto*, organ, E minor, Clavier-Übung (1729)
BWV803	*Duetto*, organ, F major, Clavier-Übung (1729)
BWV804	*Duetto*, organ, G major, Clavier-Übung (1729)
BWV805	*Duetto*, organ, A minor, Clavier-Übung (1729)
BWV806	*English Suite*, A major (c.1715)
BWV807	*English Suite*, A minor (c.1715)
BWV808	*English Suite*, G minor (c.1715)
BWV809	*English Suite*, F major (c.1715)
BWV810	*English Suite*, E minor (c.1715)
BWV811	*English Suite*, D minor (c.1715)
BWV812	*French Suite*, D minor, Clavier-Büchlein, i, for Anna Magdalena Bach (1722)
BWV813	*French Suite*, C minor, Clavier-Büchlein, i, for Anna Magdalena Bach (1722)
BWV814	*French Suite*, B minor, Clavier-Büchlein, i, for Anna Magdalena Bach (1722)
BWV815	*French Suite*, E flat major, Clavier-Büchlein, i, for Anna Magdalena Bach (1722)
BWV816	*French Suite*, G major, Clavier-Büchlein, i, for Anna Magdalena Bach (1722)
BWV817	*French Suite*, E major, Clavier-Büchlein, i, for Anna Magdalena Bach (1722)
BWV818	*Suite*, keyboard, A minor (c.1722)
BWV819	*Suite*, keyboard, E flat major (c.1722)
BWV820	*Ouverture*, keyboard, F major (1708–14)
BWV821	*Suite*, keyboard, B flat major (1708–14)
BWV822	*Suite*, keyboard, G minor
BWV823	*Suite*, keyboard, F minor (1708–14)
BWV825	*Partita*, keyboard, B flat major (1726–31)
BWV826	*Partita*, keyboard, C minor (1726–31)
BWV827	*Partita*, keyboard, A minor (1726–31)
BWV828	*Partita*, keyboard, D major (1726–31)
BWV829	*Partita*, keyboard, G major (1726–31)
BWV830	*Partita*, keyboard, E minor (1726–31)
BWV831	*Ouvertüre* [Partita] *nach französischer Art*, B minor, Clavier-Übung, ii (1735)
BWV832	*Partie*, keyboard, A major (1708–14)
BWV833	*Prelude and partita*, keyboard, F major (1708–14)

BWV836   *Allemande*, G minor, Clavier-Büchlein for W.F. Bach (1720–)
BWV837   *Allemande*, G minor, Clavier-Büchlein for W.F. Bach (1720–)
BWV841   *Minuet*, G major, Clavier-Büchlein for W.F. Bach (1720–)
BWV842   *Minuet*, G minor, Clavier-Büchlein for W.F. Bach (1720–)
BWV843   *Minuet*, G major, Clavier-Büchlein for W.F. Bach (1720–)

Das wohltemperirte Clavier, i (1722)
BWV846   *Prelude and fugue*, C major
BWV847   *Prelude and fugue*, C minor
BWV848   *Prelude and fugue*, C sharp major
BWV849   *Prelude and fugue*, C sharp minor
BWV850   *Prelude and fugue*, D major
BWV851   *Prelude and fugue*, D minor
BWV853   *Prelude and fugue*, E flat/D sharp minor
BWV854   *Prelude and fugue*, E major
BWV855   *Prelude and fugue*, E minor
BWV856   *Prelude and fugue*, F major
BWV857   *Prelude and fugue*, F minor
BWV858   *Prelude and fugue*, F sharp major
BWV859   *Prelude and fugue*, F sharp minor
BWV860   *Prelude and fugue*, G major
BWV861   *Prelude and fugue*, G minor
BWV862   *Prelude and fugue*, A flat major
BWV863   *Prelude and fugue*, G sharp minor
BWV864   *Prelude and fugue*, A major
BWV865   *Prelude and fugue*, A minor
BWV866   *Prelude and fugue*, B flat major
BWV867   *Prelude and fugue*, B flat minor
BWV868   *Prelude and fugue*, B major
BWV869   *Prelude and fugue*, B minor

Das wohltemperirte Clavier, ii (1738–42)
BWV870   *Prelude and fugue*, C major
BWV871   *Prelude and fugue*, C minor
BWV872   *Prelude and fugue*, C sharp major
BWV873   *Prelude and fugue*, C sharp minor
BWV874   *Prelude and fugue*, D major
BWV875   *Prelude and fugue*, D minor
BWV876   *Prelude and fugue*, E flat major
BWV877   *Prelude and fugue*, E flat/D sharp minor
BWV878   *Prelude and fugue*, E major
BWV879   *Prelude and fugue*, E minor
BWV880   *Prelude and fugue*, F major
BWV881   *Prelude and fugue*, F minor
BWV882   *Prelude and fugue*, F sharp major
BWV883   *Prelude and fugue*, F sharp minor
BWV884   *Prelude and fugue*, G major
BWV885   *Prelude and fugue*, G minor
BWV886   *Prelude and fugue*, A flat major

BWV887	*Prelude and fugue*, G sharp minor
BWV888	*Prelude and fugue*, A major
BWV889	*Prelude and fugue*, A minor
BWV890	*Prelude and fugue*, B flat major
BWV891	*Prelude and fugue*, B flat minor
BWV892	*Prelude and fugue*, B major
BWV893	*Prelude and fugue*, B minor

—

BWV894	*Prelude and fugue*, keyboard, A minor (1708–17)
BWV896	*Prelude and fugue*, keyboard, A major (c.1709)
BWV900	*Prelude and fughetta*, keyboard, E minor (c.1720)
BWV901	*Prelude and fughetta*, keyboard, F major
BWV902	*Prelude and fughetta*, keyboard, G major
BWV903	*Chromatic fantasia and fugue*, keyboard, D minor (c.1720)
BWV904	*Fantasia and fugue*, keyboard, A minor (c.1725)
BWV906	*Fantasia and fugue*, keyboard, C minor (c.1738)
BWV910	*Toccata*, keyboard, F sharp minor (c.1717)
BWV911	*Toccata*, keyboard, C minor (c.1717)
BWV912	*Toccata*, keyboard, D major (c.1710)
BWV913	*Toccata*, keyboard, D minor (before 1708)
BWV914	*Toccata*, keyboard, E minor (before 1708)
BWV915	*Toccata*, keyboard, G minor (before 1708)
BWV916	*Toccata*, keyboard, G major (c.1719)

Clavier-Büchlein for W.F. Bach (1720–)

BWV924	*Praeambulum*, C major
BWV926	*Prelude*, D minor
BWV927	*Praeambulum*, F major
BWV928	*Prelude*, F major
BWV929	*Trio*, G minor
BWV930	*Praeambulum*, G minor
BWV933	*Little Prelude*, C major
BWV934	*Little Prelude*, C minor

Clavier-Büchlein for Anna Magdalena Bach (1722–25)

BWV935	*Little Prelude*, D minor
BWV936	*Little Prelude*, D major
BWV937	*Little Prelude*, E major
BWV938	*Little Prelude*, E minor
BWV939	*Prelude*, C major
BWV940	*Prelude*, D minor
BWV941	*Prelude*, E minor
BWV942	*Prelude*, A minor
BWV943	*Prelude*, C major

—

BWV944	*Fugue*, keyboard, A minor
BWV946	*Fugue*, keyboard, C major (c.1708)
BWV950	*Fugue on theme by Albinoni*, keyboard, A major (c.1710)
BWV951	*Fugue on theme by Albinoni*, keyboard, B minor (c.1710)

BWV953	*Fugue*, C major, Clavier-Büchlein for W.F. Bach (1720–)
BWV954	*Fugue*, keyboard, B flat major
BWV955	*Fugue*, keyboard, B flat major
BWV958	*Fugue*, keyboard, A minor (c.1710)
BWV959	*Fugue*, keyboard, A minor (c.1710)
BWV963	*Sonata*, keyboard, D major (c.1704)
BWV965	*Sonata*, keyboard, A minor
BWV966	*Sonata*, keyboard, C major
BWV967	*Sonata*, keyboard, A minor
BWV971	*Concerto nach italiänischen Gusto* (*Italian Concerto*), Clavier-Übung, ii (1735)
BWV972	*Concerto*, keyboard, D major (1708–17)
BWV973	*Concerto*, keyboard, G major (1708–17)
BWV974	*Concerto*, keyboard, D minor (1708–17)
BWV975	*Concerto*, keyboard, G minor (1708–17)
BWV976	*Concerto*, keyboard, C major (1708–17)
BWV977	*Concerto*, keyboard, C major (1708–17)
BWV978	*Concerto*, keyboard, F major (1708–17)
BWV979	*Concerto*, keyboard, B minor (1708–17)
BWV980	*Concerto*, keyboard, G major (1708–17)
BWV981	*Concerto*, keyboard, C minor (1708–17)
BWV982	*Concerto*, keyboard, B flat major (1708–17)
BWV983	*Concerto*, keyboard, G minor (1708–17)
BWV984	*Concerto*, keyboard, C major (1708–17)
BWV985	*Concerto*, keyboard, G minor (1708–17)
BWV986	*Concerto*, keyboard, G major (1708–17)
BWV987	*Concerto*, keyboard, D minor (1708–17)
BWV988	*Aria mit verschiededenen Veraederungen* (*Goldberg Variations*), Clavier-Übung, iv (1741–42)
BWV989	*Aria variata*, A minor, (before 1714)
BWV991	*Air with variations*, C minor, Clavier-Büchlein, i, for Anna Magdalena Bach (1722)
BWV992	*Capriccio sopra la lontananza del suo fratello dilettissimo* (*Capriccio on the departure of his Most Beloved Brother*), B flat major (?1703, 1704 or 1706)
BWV993	*Capriccio*, keyboard, E major (c.1704)
BWV994	*Applicatio*, C major, Clavier-Büchlein for W.F. Bach (1720–)
BWV995	*Suite*, lute, G minor (1727–31)
BWV996	*Suite*, lute, E minor (c.1708–17)
BWV997	*Partita*, lute, C minor (1737–41)
BWV998	*Prelude*, fugue and allegro, lute, E flat major (1740s)
BWV999	*Prelude*, lute, C minor (c.1720)
BWV1000	*Fugue*, lute, G minor (c.1725)
BWV1001	*Sonata No.1*, solo violin, G minor (1720)
BWV1002	*Partita No.1*, solo violin, B minor (1720)
BWV1003	*Sonata No.2*, solo violin, A minor (1720)
BWV1004	*Partita No.2*, solo violin, D minor (1720)
BWV1005	*Sonata No.3*, solo violin, C major (1720)
BWV1006	*Partita No.3*, solo violin, E major (1720)
BWV1006a	*Partita*, lute, E major (1720)

BWV1007	*Suite*, solo violin, G major (c.1720)
BWV1008	*Suite*, solo violin, D minor (c.1720)
BWV1009	*Suite*, solo violin, C major (c.1720)
BWV1010	*Suite*, solo violin, E flat major (c.1720)
BWV1011	*Suite*, solo violin, C minor (c.1720)
BWV1012	*Suite*, solo violin, D major (c.1720)
BWV1013	*Partita*, flute, A minor (1720s)
BWV1014	*Sonata No.1*, violin and harpsichord, B minor (1717–23)
BWV1015	*Sonata No.2*, violin and harpsichord, A major (1717–23)
BWV1016	*Sonata No.3*, violin and harpsichord, E major (1717–23)
BWV1017	*Sonata No.4*, violin and harpsichord, C minor (1717–23)
BWV1018	*Sonata No.5*, violin and harpsichord, F minor (1717–23)
BWV1019	*Sonata No.6*, violin and harpsichord, G major (1717–23)
BWV1021	*Sonata*, violin and basso continuo, G major (before 1720)
BWV1023	*Sonata*, violin and basso continuo, E minor (1714–17)
BWV1027	*Sonata*, harpsichord and viola da gamba, G major (c.1720)
BWV1027a	*Trio*, organ, G major
BWV1028	*Sonata*, harpsichord and viola da gamba, D major (c.1720)
BWV1029	*Sonata*, harpsichord and viola da gamba, G minor (c.1720)
BWV1030	*Sonata*, flute and harpsichord, B minor (1730s)
BWV1032	*Sonata*, flute and harpsichord, A major (1717–23)
BWV1034	*Sonata*, flute and basso continuo, E minor (1717–20)
BWV1035	*Sonata*, flute and basso continuo, E major (1717–20)
BWV1039	*Trio Sonata*, G major (c.1720)
BWV1040	*Trio*, F major (1713)
BWV1041	*Violin Concerto*, A minor (1717–23)
BWV1042	*Violin Concerto*, E major (1717–23)
BWV1043	*Double Violin Concerto*, D minor (1717–23)
BWV1044	*Concerto*, A minor (1730s)
BWV1045	*Concerto movement for violin*, D major
BWV1046	*Brandenburg Concerto No.1*, F major (1717)
BWV1046a	*Sinfonia*, F major (1713)
BWV1047	*Brandenburg Concerto No.2*, F major (1717–18)
BWV1048	*Brandenburg Concerto No.3*, G major (1711–13)
BWV1049	*Brandenburg Concerto No.4*, G major (c.1720)
BWV1050	*Brandenburg Concerto No.5*, D major (1720–21)
BWV1051	*Brandenburg Concerto No.6*, B flat major (1708–10)
BWV1052	*Harpsichord Concerto*, D minor (1735–40)
BWV1053	*Harpsichord Concerto*, E major (1735–40)
BWV1054	*Harpsichord Concerto*, D major (1735–40)
BWV1055	*Harpsichord Concerto*, A major (1735–40)
BWV1056	*Harpsichord Concerto*, F minor (1735–40)
BWV1057	*Harpsichord Concerto*, F major (1735–40)
BWV1058	*Harpsichord Concerto*, G minor (1735–40)
BWV1059	*Harpsichord Concerto*, D minor (1735–40)
BWV1060	*Harpsichord Concerto*, C minor (1735–40)
BWV1061	*Harpsichord Concerto*, C major (1735–40)
BWV1062	*Harpsichord Concerto*, C minor (1735–40)
BWV1063	*Harpsichord Concerto*, D minor (1735–40)
BWV1064	*Harpsichord Concerto*, C major (1735–40)

BWV1065	*Harpsichord Concerto*, A minor (1735–40)	
BWV1066	*Orchestral suite*, C major (c.1717–23)	
BWV1067	*Orchestral suite*, B minor (1730s)	
BWV1068	*Orchestral suite*, D major (1730s)	
BWV1069	*Orchestral suite*, D major (c.1717–23)	
BWV1070	*Overture*, G minor	
BWV1072	*Canon trias harmonica* (1713)	
BWV1073	*Canon a 4 perpetuus* (1713)	
BWV1074	*Canon a 4* (1727)	
BWV1075	*Canon a 2 perpetuus* (1734)	
BWV1076	*Canon triplex a 6*	
BWV1077	*Canone doppio sopr'il soggetto* (1747)	
BWV1078	*Canon super fa mi a 7 post tempus musicum* (1749)	
BWV1079	*Musikalisches Opfer* (1747)	
BWV1080	*Die Kunst der Fuge* (c.1745–50)	
BWV1083	*Credo* (c.1740)	
BWV1086	*Canon concordia discors*	
BWV1087	[*14*] *Verschiedene Canones* (1742–46)	

A1–5	Fragments of church cantatas
A6–13, 18–19	Fragments of secular cantatas
A14–17, 20	Church cantatas (Lost)

SUGGESTED FURTHER READING:

- F. Blume: *Two Centuries of Bach* (Kassel, 1947; English trans. 1950)
- Malcolm Boyd: *Bach: Brandenburg Concertos* (Cambridge University Press, 1993)
- Jan Chiapusso: *Bach's World* (Indiana University Press, 1968)
- H.T. David & A. Mendel: *The Bach Reader* (New York, 1945)
- A.E.F. Dickinson: *The Art of J.S. Bach* (London 1935, rev. edition 1950)
- Imogen Holst: *Bach* (Faber, 1965)
- Malcolm Macdonald: *Bach* (Dent 'Master Musicians', 1982)
- Daniel Melamed: *J.S. Bach and the German Motet* (Cambridge University Press, 1995)
- C.H. Parry: *Johann Sebastian Bach* (Putnam, 1909)
- C.S. Terry: *Bach: A Biography* (London 1928)
- C.S. Terry: *The Music of Bach* (London 1933)
- Hannsdieter Wohlfarth: *Johann Sebastian Bach* (Fortress Press, Philadelphia, 1985)
- Percy M. Young: *The Bachs 1500–1850* (London 1970)

J.S. BACH:
RECOMMENDED RECORDINGS

The recordings listed below are all available at the time of writing. All numbers given are those that apply to the compact disc format, but many recordings can also be bought on conventional tape cassette.

The suggestions here represent inevitably only a selection from the many good recordings available, on the basis of personal response and experience, but need only be taken as a guide.

ORCHESTRAL WORKS

BWV 1046–51   **Brandenburg Concertos Nos.1–6**
♦   ASMF, Marriner   ⊗ Philips 400 076/7-2 (2)
♦   E. Concert, Pinnock   ⊗ DG Dig. 410 500/1-2

Flute concertos
BWV 1055   **Flute Concerto in C major**
BWV 1059 / BWV 35   **Flute Concerto in E minor**
BWV 1056   **Flute Concerto in G minor**
BWV 209   **Sinfonia (from Cantata No.209)**
♦   Rampal. Ars Redivivia, Munclinger   ⊗ Sony Dig. MDK 46510

Harpsichord concertos
BWV 1052   **No.1 in D minor**
BWV 1053   **No.2 in E major**
BWV 1054   **No.3 in D major**
BWV 1055   **No.4 in A major**
BWV 1056   **No.5 in F major**

BWV 1057   No.6 in F major
BWV 1058   No.7 in G minor
♦   E. Concert, Pinnock ⊗ DG Dig. 415 991-2 (Nos.1-3);
    415 992-2 (4-7)

Harpsichord concertos
BWV 1053   No.2 in E major
BWV 1055   No.4 in A major
BWV 1061   Double Harpsichord Concerto in C major
BWV 1063   Triple Harpsichord Concerto No.1 in
           D minor
♦   Leppard, Davis, Ledger, ECO, Leppard ⊗ Philips 426 084-2

Harpsichord concertos
BWV 1054   No.3 in D major
BWV 1057   No.6 in F major
BWV 1058   No.7 in G minor
BWV 1062   Double Harpsichord Concerto No.3 in
           C minor
♦   Leppard, Ledger, ECO, Leppard ⊗ Philips 426 448-2

Double harpsichord concertos
BWV 1060   No.1 in C minor
BWV 1061   No.2 in C major
BWV 1062   No.3 in C minor
♦   Pinnock, Gilbert, E. Concert ⊗ DG Dig. 415 131-2

Triple/quadruple harpsichord concertos
BWV 1063–64 Triple Harpsichord Concertos Nos.1–2
BWV 1065   Quadruple Harpsichord Concerto in
           A minor
♦   Pinnock, Gilbert, Martensen, Kraemer, E. Concert
    ⊗ DG Dig. 400 041-2

Double/triple/quadruple harpsichord concertos
BWV 1055   Harpsichord Concerto No.4 in A major
BWV 1060–62 Double Harpsichord Concertos Nos.1–3
BWV 1063–64 Triple Harpsichord Concertos Nos.1–2
BWV 1065   Quadruple Harpsichord Concerto in
           A minor

♦ Koopman and soloists, Amsterdam Bar. O. ⊗ Erato Dig. 4509 91929-2 (2)

Clavier concertos
BWV 1052–58 Nos.1–7
♦ Schiff (pf), COE ⊗ Decca Dig. 425 676-2 (2)

Clavier concertos
BWV 1052 No.1 in D minor
BWV 1053 No.2 in E major
BWV 1054 No.3 in D major
♦ Chang (pf), Cassovia, Stankovsky ⊗ Naxos Dig. 8.550422

Clavier concertos
BWV 1055 No.4 in A major
BWV 1056 No.5 in F minor
BWV 1057 No.6 in F minor
BWV 1058 No.7 in G minor
♦ Chang (pf), Cassovia, Stankovsky ⊗ Naxos Dig. 8.550423

Oboe concertos
BWV 1055 in A major
BWV 1059 in D minor
BWV 1053 in E major
♦ Holliger, ASMF, Brown ⊗ Philips Dig 415 851-2
♦ Boyd, COE ⊗ DG Dig. 429 225-2

Organ concertos
BWV 146/1052 No.1 in D minor
BWV 49/169/1053 No.2 in D major
BWV 35/1059 No.3 in D minor
BWV 1045 Sinfonia in D major
BWV 29 Cantata
♦ Sinfonia (reconstructed and ed. Schurck) Hurford, N. Sinfonia, Hickox ⊗ Argo Dig. 425 479-2, 425, 497-4

Violin concertos
BWV 1041[1] No.1 in A minor
BWV 1042[2] No.2 in E major
BWV 1043[3] Double Violin Concerto in D minor

BWV 1060[4]   **Double Concerto for Violin & Oboe in D minor**

♦ [3]Grumiaux; Krebbers, [4]Holliger; [1-3]Les Solistes Romandes, Gerecz; [4]New Philh. O, de Waart ⊗ Philips 420 700-2

♦ Kremer; [4]Holliger; ASMF ⊗ Philips Dig. 432 0036-2.

Violin concertos

BWV 1041   **No.1 in A minor**
BWV 1042   **No.2 in E major**
BWV 1043   **Double Violin Concerto in D minor**
BWV 1064   **Triple Violin Concerto in D major**

♦ Wallfisch, Bury, Beznosink, Mackintosh, O. of Age of Enlightenment ⊗ Virgin / EMI Dig. VC7 59319-2

Violin concertos

BWV 1041   **No.1 in A minor**
BWV 1042   **No.2 in E major**
BWV 1043[1]   **Double Violin Concerto in D minor**
BWV 1060[2]   **Violin and Oboe Concerto in C minor**

♦ [1]Garcia (vn); [2]Black (ob); ECO, Sitkovetsky (vn) ⊗ Novalis 150 017-2

BWV 1079   **The Musical Offering**

♦ ASMF, Marriner ⊗ Philips 412 800-2

BWV 1079   **The Musical Offering**
BWV 1067   **Suite No.2 in B minor**

♦ Stuttgart CO, Münchinger; Rampal ⊗ Decca 430 266-2; 430 266-4

Orchestral suites

BWV 1066   **No.1 in C major**
BWV 1067   **No.2 in B minor**
BWV 1068   **No.3 in D major**
BWV 1069   **No.4 in D major**

♦ ASMF, Marriner ⊗ Decca 430 378-2; 430 378-4

♦ AAM, Hogwood ⊗ O-L Dig. 417 834-2

BWV 1066–9   **Orchestral Suites Nos.1–4**
BWV 1079   **The Musical Offering**

♦ ASMF, Marriner ⊗ Decca 430 378-2
♦ E. Bar. Soloists, Gardiner ⊗ Erato / Warner Dig. 4509 91800-2 (2)

BWV 1080   The Art of Fugue (orchestral version)
♦ Musica Antiqua Cologne, Goebel ⊗ Archiv 413 642-2

CHAMBER MUSIC

Cello suites
BWV 1007   No.1 in G major
BWV 1008   No.2 in D minor
BWV 1009   No.3 in C major
BWV 1010   No.4 in E major
BWV 1011   No.5 in C minor
BWV 1012   No.6 in D minor
♦ Schiff ⊗ EMI Dig. 47471-8 (2)
♦ Gendron ⊗ Philips Duo 442 293-2 (2)
♦ Kirschbaum ⊗ Virgin / EMI Dig. VCD5 45086-2 (2)

Flute sonatas
BWV 1030–5   Nos.1–6
BWV 1020   in G minor
BWV 1027–29   Viola da Gamba Sonatas Nos.1–3
♦ Larrieu, Puyana, Kuijken; Cervera, Puyana ⊗ Philips Duo 438 809-2 (2)

Flute sonatas
BWV 1030–5   Nos.1–6
BWV 1020   in G minor
BWV 1013   Partita in A minor
♦ Preston, Pinnock, Savall ⊗ CRD 3314/5 (2)

Lute suites (arr. for guitar)
BWV 995   No.1 in G minor
BWV 996   No.2 in E minor
BWV 997   Partita in C minor
BWV 1006a   Partita in E major
♦ Williams (guitar) ⊗ Sony MK 42204

Trio sonatas (arr. for guitar)

BWV 1036   No.1 in D minor
BWV 1037   No.2 in C major
BWV 1038–9   Nos.3 & 4 in G minor
♦   London Baroque ⊗ HM Dig. HMC 901173, HMC 401173

Viola da Gamba sonatas

BWV 1027–9 Nos.1–3
♦   Ma (vc), Cooper ⊗ Sony Dig. MK 37794
♦   Kuijken, Leonhardt ⊗ HM/BMG GD 77044

Sonatas and partitas for solo violin

BWV 1001, 1003, 1005   Violin Sonatas Nos.1–3
BWV 1002, 1004, 1006   Violin Partitas Nos.1–3
♦   Grumiaux ⊗ Philips Duo 438 736-2 (2)
♦   Perlman ⊗ EMI Dig. CD57 49483-2 (2)

Violin sonatas (for violin and harpsichord)

BWV 1014–9   Nos.1–6
♦   Kuijken, Leonhardt ⊗ HM/BMG GD 77150 (2)

Sonatas for violin and continuo

BWV 1020–4   Sonatas for Violin and Continuo
BWV 1014–9   Violin Sonatas Nos.1–6
♦   Grumiaux, Jaccottet, Mermaud ⊗ Philips 426 452-2;
426 452-4 (2)

KEYBOARD WORKS (EXCLUDING WORKS FOR ORGAN)

BWV 1080   The Art of Fugue
♦   Gilbert (hpd) ⊗ DG Dig. 427 673-2

BWV 1080   The Art of Fugue
BWV 971   Italian Concerto
BWV 831   Partita in B minor
BWV 998   Prelude, Fugue and Allegro in E major
♦   Leonhardt (hpd) ⊗ HM/BMG GD 77013 (2)

BWV 903   Chromatic Fantasia and Fugue in D minor

BWV 906	Fantasia in C minor
BWV 917	Fantasia in G minor
BWV 919	Fantasia in C minor
BWV 904	Fantasia and Fugue in A minor
BWV 921	Prelude in C minor
BWV 922	Prelude in A minor
BWV 894	Prelude and Fugue in A minor
BWV 901	Prelude and Fugue in F major
BWV 902	Prelude and Fugue in G major

♦ Staier (hpd) ⊗ HM/BMG RD 77039

Toccatas

BWV 910	F sharp minor
BWV 911	C minor
BWV 912	D major
BWV 913	D minor
BWV 914	E minor
BWV 915	G minor
BWV 916	G major

♦ van Asperen (hpd) ⊗ EMI Dig. CDC7 54081-2
♦ Rübsam (pf) ⊗ Naxos Dig. 8.550708
♦ Gould (pf) ⊗ Sony SM2K 52612 (2)

BWV 802–5   **4 Duets**
♦ Rübsam (pf) ⊗ Naxos Dig.8.550930

BWV 806–11   **English Suites Nos.1–6**
♦ Schiff (pf) ⊗ Decca Dig. 421 640-2 (2)

BWV 812–7   **French Suites Nos.1–6**
♦ Leonhardt (hpd) ⊗ RCA GD71963
♦ Koopman (hpd) ⊗ Erato / Warner Dig. 4509 94805-2
♦ MacGregor (pf) ⊗ Collins Dig. 1371-2

BWV 812–7   **French Suites Nos.1–6**
BWV 831   **French Overture**
♦ Gould (pf) ⊗ Sony SM2K52609

BWV 988   **Goldberg Variations**
♦ van Asperen (hpd) ⊗ EMI Dig. CDC7 54209-2

- Landowska (hpd) ⊗ EMI CDH7 61008-2
- Gould (pf) ⊗ Sony Dig. SMK 52619
- Tureck (pf) ⊗ VAI Audio VAIA 1029

| BWV 772–86 | **15 2-part Inventions** |
| BWV 787–801 | **15 3-part Inventions** |

- Koopman (hpd) ⊗ Capriccio Dig. 10 210 (includes 6 Little Preludes)
- Schiff (pf) ⊗ Decca Dig. 411 974-2

| BWV 825–30 | **Partitas Nos.1–6** |

- Schiff (pf) ⊗ Decca Dig. 411 732-2 (2)
- Rousset (hpd) ⊗ Oiseau-Lyre Dig. 440 217-2 (2)

| BWV 846–93 | **The Well-Tempered Clavier (Books 1 & 2)** |

- Gilbert (hpd) ⊗ DG Dig. 413 439-2 (4)
- Schiff (pf) ⊗ Decca Dig. 414 388-2

WORKS FOR ORGAN

There is a vast array of recordings of Bach's huge output for the organ. For convenience the following listings include three recommended recording cycles of the complete organ works, together with a short selection of notable recordings of specific groups of works.

Complete organ works

12-volume set (12 discs)

- Rogg ⊗ Harmonia Mundi HMX 290772
- Rogg ⊗ Harmonia Mundi HMX 290773
- Rogg ⊗ Harmonia Mundi HMX 290774
- Rogg ⊗ Harmonia Mundi HMX 290775/6
- Rogg ⊗ Harmonia Mundi HMX 290777
- Rogg ⊗ Harmonia Mundi HMX 290778/9
- Rogg ⊗ Harmonia Mundi HMX 290780
- Rogg ⊗ Harmonia Mundi HMX 290781/2
- Rogg ⊗ Harmonia Mundi HMX 290783

4-volume set (16 discs)
♦ Rübsam ⊗ Philips 438 170-2 (16)

6-volume set (17 discs)
♦ Hurford ⊗ Decca 421 337-2 (3)
♦ Hurford ⊗ Decca 421 341-2 (3)
♦ Hurford ⊗ Decca 421 617-2 (3)
♦ Hurford ⊗ Decca Dig. / Analogue 421 621-2 (3)
♦ Hurford ⊗ Decca 425 631-2 (3)
♦ Hurford ⊗ Decca 425 635-2 (2)

Groups of organ works
BWV 525–30   Six Trio Sonatas
♦ Preston ⊗ DG Dig. 437 835-2
♦ Herrick ⊗ Hyperion Dig. CDA 66390

BWV 1080   The Art of Fugue (organ version)
♦ Alain ⊗ Erato / Warner Dig. 4509 91946-2

Organ partitas
BWV 766   Christ, der du bist der helle Tag
BWV 767   O Gott, du frommer Gott
BWV 768   Sei gegrüsset, Jesu gütig
BWV 770   Ach, was soll ich Sünder machen?
♦ Preston ⊗ DG 429 775-2GH

BWV 565   Toccata and Fugue in D minor
BWV 540   Toccata and Fugue in F major
BWV 538   Toccata and Fugue in D minor, 'Dorian'
BWV 564   Toccata, Adagio and Fugue in C major
BWV 582   Passacaglia and Fugue in C minor
♦ Herrick ⊗ Hyperion CDA 66434

BWV 599–644   Orgel-Büchlein
♦ Preston (org.) ⊗ DG Dig. 431 816-2

BWV 714 / 719 /   35 Arnstadt
957 / 742 / 1090–1120 chorale preludes
BWV 639   Chorale Prelude: Ich Ruf' zu dir
BWV 531   Prelude and Fugue in C major

BWV 549a Prelude and Fugue in D minor
BWV 535   Prelude and Fugue in G minor
BWV 566   Prelude and Fugue in E major
♦ Barber (org.) ⊗ ASV Gaudeamus Dig. CD GAU 120/121 (available separately)

BWV 553–6 8 Little Preludes and Fugues
BWV 532   Prelude and Fugue in D major
BWV 564   Toccata, Adagio and Fugue in C major
BWV 525   Trio Sonata No.1 in E flat major
♦ Koopman (org.) ⊗ ASV Novalis Dig. 150 066-2

BWV 645–50 6 Schübler Chorales
BWV 590   Pastorale in F major
BWV 582   Passacaglia in C minor
BWV 564   Toccata, Adagio and Fugue in C major
BWV 565   Toccata and Fugue in D minor
♦ Koopman (org.) ⊗ DG Dig. 427 801-2; 427 801-4

VOCAL AND CHORAL WORKS

There are numerous recordings of Bach's vast output of cantatas. The following listing includes the only recording of the complete cantatas, together with a short selection of notable recordings of the secular cantatas. For reasons of space, the cantatas are designated only by their BWV numbers; full designations are given in the listing of complete works (see pages 67–89).

Complete cantatas
Teldec / Warner: Harnoncourt / Leonhardt recording cycle (various ensembles):
45-volume set (83 discs)

BWV 1–4   Cantatas
♦ ⊗ Teldec / Warner 2292 42497-2 (2)
BWV 5–8   Cantatas
♦ ⊗ Teldec / Warner 2292 42498-2 (2)
BWV 9–11 Cantatas
♦ ⊗ Teldec / Warner 2292 42499-2 (2)

BWV 12–16   **Cantatas**
♦   ⊗ Teldec / Warner 2292 42500-2 (2)

BWV 17–20   **Cantatas**
♦   ⊗ Teldec / Warner 2292 42501-2 (2)

BWV 21–23   **Cantatas**
♦   ⊗ Teldec / Warner 2292 42502-2 (2)

BWV 24–27   **Cantatas**
♦   ⊗ Teldec / Warner 2292 42503-2 (2)

BWV 28–30   **Cantatas**
♦   ⊗ Teldec / Warner 2292 42504-2 (2)

BWV 31–34   **Cantatas**
♦   ⊗ Teldec / Warner 2292 42505-2 (2)

BWV 35–38   **Cantatas**
♦   ⊗ Teldec / Warner 2292 42506-2 (2)

BWV 39–42   **Cantatas**
♦   ⊗ Teldec / Warner 2292 42556-2 (2)

BWV 43–46   **Cantatas**
♦   ⊗ Teldec / Warner 2292 42559-2 (2)

BWV 47–50   **Cantatas**
♦   ⊗ Teldec / Warner 2292 42560-2 (2)

BWV 51–56   **Cantatas**
♦   ⊗ Teldec / Warner 2292 42422-2 (2)

BWV 57–60   **Cantatas**
♦   ⊗ Teldec / Warner 2292 42423-2

BWV61–64   **Cantatas**
♦   ⊗ Teldec / Warner 2292 42565-2 (2)

BWV 65–68   **Cantatas**
♦   ⊗ Teldec / Warner 2292 42571-2 (2)

BWV 69–72   **Cantatas**
♦   ⊗ Teldec / Warner 2292 42572-2 (2)

BWV 73–75   **Cantatas**
♦   ⊗ Teldec / Warner 2292 42573-2

BWV 76–79   **Cantatas**
♦   ⊗ Teldec / Warner 2292 42576-2 (2)

BWV 80–83   **Cantatas**
♦   ⊗ Teldec / Warner 2292 42577-2 (2)

BWV 84–90   **Cantatas**
♦   ⊗ Teldec / Warner 2292 42578-2 (2)

BWV 91–94   **Cantatas**
♦   ⊗ Teldec / Warner 2292 42582-2 (2)

BWV 95–98   Cantatas
♦   ⊗ Teldec / Warner 2292 42583-2
BWV 99–102   Cantatas
♦   ⊗ Teldec / Warner 2292 42584-2 (2)
BWV 103–106   Cantatas
♦   ⊗ Teldec / Warner 2292 42602-2
BWV 107–110   Cantatas
♦   ⊗ Teldec / Warner 2292 42603-2 (2)
BWV 111–114   Cantatas
♦   ⊗ Teldec / Warner 2292 42606-2 (2)
BWV 115–117, 119   Cantatas
♦   ⊗ Teldec / Warner 2292 42608-2 (2)
BWV 120–123   Cantatas
♦   ⊗ Teldec / Warner 2292 42609-2 (2)
BWV 124–127   Cantatas
♦   ⊗ Teldec / Warner 2292 42615-2
BWV 128–131   Cantatas
♦   ⊗ Teldec / Warner 2292 42617-2 (2)
BWV 132–135   Cantatas
♦   ⊗ Teldec / Warner 2292 42618-2 (2)
BWV 136–139   Cantatas
♦   ⊗ Teldec / Warner 2292 42619-2
BWV 140, 143–146   Cantatas
♦   ⊗ Teldec / Warner Dig. 2292 42630-2 (2)
BWV 147–151   Cantatas
♦   ⊗ Teldec / Warner Dig. 2292 42631-2 (2)
BWV 152–156   Cantatas
♦   ⊗ Teldec / Warner Dig. 2292 42632-2 (2)
BWV 157–159, 161–163   Cantatas
♦   ⊗ Teldec / Warner Dig. 2292 42633-2 (2)
BWV 164–169   Cantatas
♦   ⊗ Teldec / Warner Dig. 292 42634-2 (2)
BWV 170–174   Cantatas
♦   ⊗ Teldec / Warner Dig. 2292 42635-2 (2)
BWV 175–179   Cantatas
♦   ⊗ Teldec / Warner Dig. 2292 42428-2 (2)
BWV 180–184   Cantatas
♦   ⊗ Teldec / Warner Dig. 2292 42738-2 (2)
BWV 185–188   Cantatas
♦   ⊗ Teldec / Warner Dig. 2292 44179-2 (2)

BWV 192, 194, 195   Cantatas
♦   ⊗ Teldec / Warner Dig. 2292 44193-2
BWV 196–199   Cantatas
♦   ⊗ Teldec / Warner Dig. 2292 44194-2 (2)

Secular cantatas
Cantatas BWV 202 'Wedding' Cantata, BWV 209[1], BWV 211[1,2,3] 'Coffee' Cantata, BWV 212[1,2,3] 'Peasant' Cantata
♦   [1]Ameling (sop); [2]English (ten); [3]Nimsgern (bass); Collegium Aureum   ⊗ DHM GD77151. From BASF BAC3052/3 (9/74)

Cantatas BWV 206, 207a
♦   Ziesak, Chance, Prégardien, Kooy, Stuttgart Ch. Choir, Cologne   ⊗ Sony SK46492

Cantatas BWV 205, 214
♦   Van der Sluis, Jacobs, Prégardien, Thomas, Age of Enlightenment Ch. & O., Leonhardt   ⊗ Philips Dig. 432 161-2

Cantata BWV 208 ('Hunt' Cantata)
♦   Smith, Kirkby, Davis, George, Parley of Instrumenrs, Goodman   ⊗ Hyp. Dig. CDA 66169

Cantatas BWV 211 'Coffee' Cantata, BWV 212 'Peasant' Cantata
♦   Kirkby, Roger, Covey-Crump, Thomas, AAM, Hogwood ⊗ O-L Dig. 417 621-2

Cantata BWV 249 Easter Oratorio, BWV10 Cantata
♦   Ameling, Watts, Krenn, Rintzler, Vienna Academy Ch., Stuttgart CO, Münchinger   ⊗ Decca 425 650-2

BWV 248   Christmas Oratorio
♦   Rolfe Johnson, Argenta, Von Otter, Blochwitz, Bär, Monteverdi Ch., E. Bar. Soloists, Gardiner ⊗ DG Dig. 423 232-2 (2)
BWV 248   Christmas Oratorio
BWV 243   Magnificat in D major

♦   Ameling, Watts, Pears, Krause, Ch., Stuttgart CO,
    Münchinger   ⊗ Decca 425 441-2 (3)

BWV 243   **Magnificat in D major**
BWV 51   **Cantata: Jauchzet Gott in allen landen!**
♦   Argenta, Kwella, Kirkby, Brett, Rolfe Johnson, David
    Thomas, E. Bar. Soloists, Gardiner   ⊗ Ph Dig. 411 458-2

BWV 232   **Mass in B minor**
♦   Argenta, Dawson, Fairfield, Knibbs, Kwella, Hall, Nichols,
    Chance, Collin, Stafford, Evans, Milner, Murgatroyd,
    Lloyd-Morgan, Varcoe, Monteverdi Ch., E. Bar. Soloists,
    Gardiner   ⊗ DG Dig. 415 514-2
♦   Kirkby, Van Evera, Iconomou, Immler, Kilian,
    Covey-Crump, Thomas, Taverner Consort, Taverner
    Players / Parrott   ⊗ EMI CDS7 47293-8

Masses
BWV 233   **in F major**
BWV 234   **in A major**
BWV 235   **in G minor**
BWV 236   **in G major**
♦   Bonney, Remmert, Trost, Bär, Berlin RIAS Chbr. Ch.,
    CPE Bach Chbr. O., Schreier   ⊗ Philips 438 873-2

Motets
BWV 225   **Singet dem Herrn ein neues Lied**
BWV 226   **Der Geist hilft unser Schwachheit**
BWV 227   **Jesu meine Freude**
BWV 228   **Der Gerechte kommt um Fürchte dich
          nicht**
BWV 229   **Komm, Jesu, Komm**
BWV 230   **Lobet den Herrn**
BWV 231   **Sei Lob und Preis mit Ehren**
♦   Priday, Fisher, Stafford, McKenzie, Savage,
    Monteverdi Ch., E. Bar. Soloists, Gardiner
       ⊗ Erato / Warner 2292 45979-2 (2)

BWV 245   **St. John Passion**
♦   Rolfe Johnson, Varcoe, Hauptmann, Argenta & soloists,

Monteverdi Ch., E. Bar. Soloists, Gardiner
⊗ DG Dig. 419 324-2 (2)
◆ Wunderlich, Fischer-Dieskau, Grümmer, Ludwig,
St. Hedwig's Cath. Ch., Berlin SO, Foster
⊗ EMI CZS7 64234-2 (2)
◆ Prégardien, Van der Kamp, Schlick, Jacobs, Van der Meel,
Van Egmond, La Petite Bande Ch. & O., Kuijken
⊗ BMG / RCA GD 77041 (2)

BWV 244   St. Matthew Passion
◆ Rolfe Johnson, Schmidt, Bonney, Monoyios, Von Otter,
Chance, Crook, Bär, Hauptmann, Monteverdi Ch., E. Bar.
Soloists, Gardiner ⊗ DG Dig. 427 648-2 (3)
◆ Schreier, Fischer-Dieskau, Mathis, Baker, Salminen,
Regensburger Domspätzen, Munich Bach Ch. & O.,
Richter ⊗ DG 427 704-2 (3)
◆ Pears, Fischer-Dieskau, Schwarzkopf, Ludwig, Gedda,
Berry, Hampstead Parish Church Ch., Philh. Ch. & O.,
Klemperer ⊗ EMI CMS7 63058-2 (3)

Index

CLASSIC *f*M

MUSIC

A JOY FOR LIFE

EDWARD HEATH

Foreword by Yehudi Menuhin

Music is a record of a lifetime's passion for a subject with which former Prime Minister Sir Edward Heath has been involved since he was nine years old. In this book – first published in 1976 and now updated in his eighty-first year – Sir Edward recalls his musical experiences, from his days as a chorister in his parish church to his work as a conductor of international renown – a career that began in 1971 when he conducted the London Symphony Orchestra playing Elgar's 'Cockaigne' Overture at its gala concert in the Royal Festival Hall.

From his friendships with Herbert von Karajan and Leonard Bernstein to his great musical loves such as Beethoven and British music, from music at Downing Street to a series of five symphony concerts he conducted for his eightieth birthday celebrations, Sir Edward gives a fascinating personal insight into his wide-ranging experience. Written with great knowledge and characteristic enthusiasm, *Music – A Joy for Life* will appeal both to those who already have a serious interest in music and also to those who enjoy music and would like a greater understanding.

£16.99   ISBN: 1 86205 090 2

THE
CLASSIC *f*M
GUIDE TO
CLASSICAL MUSIC

JEREMY NICHOLAS
Consultant Editor: ROBIN RAY
Foreword by HUMPHREY BURTON

'... *a fascinating and accessible guide ... it will provide*
an informative and illuminating source of insight
for everybody from the beginner to the musicologist.'

Sir Edward Heath

The Classic fM Guide to Classical Music opens with a masterly
history of classical music, illustrated with charts and lifelines, and
is followed by a comprehensive guide to more than 500 composers. There are major entries detailing the lives and works of the
world's most celebrated composers, as well as concise biographies
of more than 300 others.

This invaluable companion to classical music combines extensive factual detail with fascinating anecdotes, and an insight
into the historical and musical influences of the great composers.
It also contains reviews and recommendations of the best works,
and extensive cross-references to lesser-known composers.
Jeremy Nicholas's vibrant, informative and carefully researched
text is complemented by photographs and cartoons, and is designed for easy reference, with a comprehensive index.

£19.99 ISBN: 1 85793 760 0 Hardback
£9.99 ISBN: 1 86205 051 1 Paperback